Treatise On
Prayer And Meditation

"Let not the book of this law depart from thy mouth, but thou shalt meditate on it day and night, that thou mayst observe and do all things that are written in it. Then shalt thou direct thy way and understand it."

—Josue 1:8

St. Peter of Alcantara (1499-1562) was a famous Franciscan superior, great penitent, miracle-worker and spiritual director of St. Teresa of Avila .

Treatise On Prayer And Meditation

by

ST. PETER OF ALCANTARA

Translated with an Introduction and Sketch of the Saint's Life

by

DOMINIC DEVAS, O.F.M.

Together with a complete English version of

PAX ANIMAE

by

JOHN OF BONILLA

> *"Let thy thoughts be upon the pre-
> cepts of God, and meditate continually
> on his commandments, and he will
> give thee a heart, and the desire of wis-
> dom shall be given to thee."*
> —Ecclesiasticus 6:37

TAN BOOKS AND PUBLISHERS

Nihil Obstat: Fr. Sylvester Nash, O.F.M.
                  Censor Deputatus

Imprimi Potest: Fr. Herbertus Doyle, O.F.M.
                  Minister Angliae
                  Die 23rd Januarii, 1926

Nihil Obstat: G. H. Joyce, S.J.
                  Censor Deputatus

Imprimatur: Edm. Can. Surmont,
                  Vicarius Generalis, Westmonasterii
                  Die 29th Aprilis, 1926

Library of Congress Catalog Card No.: 86-50148

ISBN: 978-0-89555-887-9

Cover design by Milo Persic. The cover photo was taken by Milo Persic at the Cathedral of St. Paul, St. Paul MN.

Printed and bound in the United States of America.

TAN BOOKS AND PUBLISHERS
2009

DEDICATION

MOST magnificent and most devout Signor: I should never have compiled this little treatise nor consented to its publication had you not often commanded me to write something on prayer in short and compendious form, and clearly, in order to be of service to all. This inexpensive and slender volume will be accessible even to the poor, who cannot buy more expensive books, and being written clearly, will profit the simple, who are not rich in understanding. I have deemed it a matter of no slight merit, in these circumstances, to obey one who demanded of me something so holy and fitting, thinking also that the merit of a work due to so saintly a demand would be very real. I shall profit by it myself, unless indeed the very great affection and tenderness I bear to you and your spouse and companion, Doña Francisca—bound to you by the ties of charity and love in Christ Jesus, our whole Good, as [also] by those of marriage—unless, I say, this affection does not take from me some part of my merit. However, if it is true, as indeed it is, that Christians participate in the good works of their brethren, without diminishing at all thereby the merit of the latter, well may I say that I participate in your devotion and in all your good works, that you are my children, most dear to me in the Lord, and that you look on me as your father. The poverty of my doctrine and the zeal of my devotion have never failed you when there was question of your holy desires and lofty enterprises. After having read many books on this subject, I have briefly drawn out and gathered up from them what seemed to me the most profitable.[1] God grant it may thus bring help to all who seek it, because for such also is it meant. You yourselves will win from it the spiritual reward of your good intentions and I the fruit of your good will. All to the honour

---

1. In the Lisbon edition, anterior to 1559, is found at this point of the Dedication, the Saint's express reference, *among other books,* to that on Prayer *recently compiled by the very reverend Father Provincial, Brother Louis of*

and glory of Jesus Christ, our whole Good,
from whom all good proceeds.

Granada of the Friaris Preachers. From this, he writes, he
has picked out and gathered together, in compendious
[abbreviated] form, all it is necessary to know about
prayer. Père Ubald d'Alençon thus summarizes his own
conclusions on the vexed question of the authenticity of
the *Treatise on Prayer* ascribed to St. Peter: 1) The author
is certainly St. Peter, but 2) he used the larger treatise of
[Ven.] Louis of Granada, making a kind of *résumé* of it, and
giving extracts; but he acknowledges his source, a thing
quite rare in those days. 3) It was written about 1556,
probably at La Lapa (Badajoz). 4) [Ven.] Louis of Granada
augmented his original work in 1566. Later editions of St.
Peter's *Treatise* omit the reference to Louis of Granada's
work, presumably because the latter had fallen foul of the
Spanish Inquisition; as did indeed, also, this very Treatise
of St. Peter.

PUBLISHER'S PREFACE

S T. PETER OF ALCANTARA (1499-
1562), the author of *Treatise on Prayer
and Meditation*, was himself a very
holy man who, during his entire adult life, did
great penance, worked many miracles and
experienced the miraculous on a regular
basis. St. Teresa of Avila, who was a "spiritual
daughter" of St. Peter, in writing her Auto-
biography, claimed that he ate only one meal
every three days and slept only one hour
a night—and that, sitting at his desk. After
St. Peter died, he appeared to her in glory
and averred that he was very happy he had
done all that penance.

St. Peter was not a writer by profession,
other than to compose constitutions govern-
ing his branch of the Franciscan Order.
Treatise on Prayer and Meditation is his sole
book and was written only because it was
requested of him by Don Rodrigo de Chaves,
a noble patron of his, to whom he dedicated
the book; otherwise, he would never have

written it. Happy circumstance indeed! It is a
singular grace that this book was ever written. For in this little volume he summarizes
brilliantly the whole basic Catholic method
and art of mental prayer.

Reading the *Treatise,* one can easily see
that it was written by someone who was a
master of his subject as well as a master of
writing style, a highly intelligent and erudite
man, one who could very easily have distin-
guished himself as a spiritual writer, had he
chosen that field for his apostolic endeavor.
The salient qualities of St. Peter's masterful
little book are its brevity, thoroughness, intel-
ligibility, penetration, instruction, inspiration
and authority.

Though written primarily for priests and
religious, it is nonetheless great for lay people as well—for all the reasons alluded to
above: 1) It is short; 2) it covers the topic of
mental prayer very well; 3) it is easily understood; 4) it is a *profound* book, filled with
practical wisdom; 5) it is highly instructive
and didactic (educational); 6) it is highly
inspirational, especially for its meditations
(which are as good as one will find anywhere)
and also for its ability to *motivate* the reader
to engage in prayer and meditation; 7) it is
written with authority, conviction and confidence, for St. Peter's personal sanctity was a

product of the very method he advocates here.

In its own right, the life of St. Peter of Alcantara is well worth reading, even though his fame and achievements are still largely eclipsed in history by those of his spiritual daughter, St. Teresa of Avila. Yet the pre-eminent in any field themselves usually stand on the shoulders of giants—as St. Thomas Aquinas on Albertus Magnus, and they in turn on St. Augustine, Plato and Aristotle. Yet it would seem that the day will come when the brilliance of St. Peter of Alcantara's life and work will shine before the world with their own well-deserved beauty and lustre.

The *Treatise* is not just another holy book to be read for its wisdom and then set aside as the reader passes on to other great Catholic books. Rather, it should be thought of as a handbook, a guide, a roadmap for your prayer life and spiritual advancement, a book to be read, pencil in hand, marking and highlighting points that especially pertain to you personally in your quest for growth in prayer and sanctity. For here is a book replete with trusted and practical techniques to be thoroughly learned and *applied,* to be built into your own spiritual discipline. The *Treatise* should become a book-to-carry (a *vade mecum* —a "go with me") that you keep handy and consult repeatedly, until its elements are mastered. Other great spiritual books of course should also be read, but since we should all pray every day, this book should stay close at hand for assistance in praying and meditating well.

St. Peter advises that one and one-half to two hours a day be devoted to mental prayer (page 110 of the text), and the footnote says St. Teresa of Avila urges two hours per day. This will seem like a great deal of time, especially for parish priests and people living and working in the world, for mothers and fathers of minor children, for students and those working long hours. Nonetheless, this is the sort of time usually required for fruitful mental prayer, per St. Peter, St. Teresa and various other great Saints. Why is so much time needed every day? The answer is very simple: It takes the dedication of this amount of time, especially for beginners, for the mind and body to become quiet and for the mind to focus on the subject under meditation.

What is to be done in this regard by those who, because of their duties, have little time to spare for mental prayer? Some parents solve the problem by rising very early in the morning—at 4:00 or 4:30 a.m.—to engage in prayer while their families and the world in general are still asleep. Some such practice as this should be attempted by those who do not have much time, provided that the sacrifice of time and perhaps sleep does not interfere later in the day with their performing the duties required in their state of life. Those who are not able to devote one and a half to two hours to mental prayer each day, St. Peter says, should seek help from Our Lord and Our Lady to solve this problem. And as St. Peter comments, periodically giving the requisite time for this exercise will yield more fruit and help people to be more successful than trying to perform this type of prayer every day with too little time devoted to it.

St. Alphonsus Liguori (1696-1787), a Doctor of the Church and author of 111 books, many geared for the laity, maintains in a number of his popular writings that mental prayer is necessary for salvation. Why would this be so? Why would he maintain this seemingly startling position? When we consider the nature of man, and viewing man's situation in the light of our Faith, his position becomes understandable, though most of us would normally not reflect upon this truth: People most of the time act on what they think about. If we would never think about God, about our relationship with Him and about the truths of our religion (by practicing mental prayer), then our religious beliefs—if indeed we could have any correct ones under this condition—would have little or no practical effect on how we behave. Yet we know that our eternal destiny will depend on what we have done in this life and the state of our souls at the moment of death, because Our Lord Himself has told us, "For the Son of man shall come in the glory of his Father with his angels, and *then will he render to every man according to his works.*" (*Matthew* 16:27, emphasis added). In the course of our daily lives, we tend to become engrossed in what we are doing and distracted by our own busyness. Without our meditating at least periodically on the ultimate purpose of life, we can easily fall into sin, even mortal sin, because we do not have in our souls the necessary intellectual motivation to avoid it. And the more often we sin, the less seriously do we regard sin. Without at least occasional meditation on religious truths (mental prayer), our precarious situation in life vis-à-vis our own salvation would seldom if ever become to us a powerful *realization* and we could easily be lulled into a spiritual sleep from which we might never sufficiently awaken to take the necessary steps to save our souls.

In many places in his writings, St. Alphonsus also says that unless we pray, we shall not save our souls. Why is this so? He answers that it is because we need the grace of God to achieve this goal, and God will not grant us this grace unless we *ask* it of Him! Here again, if we never meditate upon and ponder over our spiritual situation in life and what it takes to save our souls, it is most likely we shall seldom if ever pray for God's help, without which, as he says, we shall be lost because we have not asked God in prayer for the necessary grace of salvation.

We should realize that all standard oral prayers have a certain amount of mental prayer built into them. This is especially true of the Rosary, which is filled with meditation content and which constitutes (if analyzed carefully) a very sophisticated prayer discipline. Thus, one cannot pray most standard Catholic prayers without doing some mental prayer, if he is at all paying attention to what he is saying in his prayers. Nonetheless, what St. Peter and other writers on the subject of mental prayer mean more specifically by mental prayer is what the author describes in the *Treatise*—that is, a purposefully and solely concentrated activity of meditation, without set formulary words, and where the mind is quite free to consider the subject under meditation in all its various aspects.

Further, a lesson that should impress your

mind as you consider carefully the advice of the *Treatise* is that either you will grow and advance in prayer and the spiritual life, or you will go backwards; there is really no middle ground. We can never be safely satisfied with where we are spiritually, or we shall regress. Our Lord says, "I would thou wert cold or hot. But because thou art lukewarm, and neither cold nor hot, I will begin to vomit thee out of my mouth." (*Apocalypse* 3:15-16). If you do not strive to grow and progress, you will go backwards. In spiritual combat, as in actual military combat, one cannot simply hold the ground he has gained, or the enemy will defeat him. For the cares and allurements of our lives, plus our natural love for ease of life (voluptuousness, or luxury), plus the habitual sins we all commit (be they ever so slight, or only imperfections)—all these factors can combine to lull our souls into a spiritual somnambulance, a dangerous spiritually semiconscious lethargy, if you will, that we may not even be totally aware of, with the result that, despite having a seemingly good prayer-life routine, we may actually be slipping backwards, rather than advancing spiritually.

St. Peter gives the remedy for this problem: It is not simply to add more oral prayer on top of all the prayers we may already be saying—especially for those living active lives in the world—so that we become burdened with hours of what we may think are our "mandatory" oral prayers. Rather, we should fight this spiritual torpor with often-repeated acts of love toward God, proceeding through our daily lives with a conscious, sublimating spiritual attitude of supernatural, sacrificial love in all that we do. The result will be a constant breaking up of any spiritual "stoniness" about our hearts or dangerous spiritual complacency that can develop (as mentioned above) as a result of the combined distractions of life, our subtle love of comfort and ease, and the dulling effects of any sins we may commit. These on-going acts of love toward God, of course, do not substitute for time devoted specifically and entirely to prayer. When Our Lord in the Garden said to the three Apostles—Peter, James and John—"Could you not watch one hour with Me," He was not addressing them only, and for just that particular occasion, but He was addressing us all, throughout all time, asking us, "Could you not give one hour of your day completely and unreservedly to Me in prayer?" For He followed this request with a warning that pertains to everyone, "Watch ye and pray, that ye enter not into temptation. The spirit indeed is willing, but the flesh weak." (*Matthew* 26:40-41).

Shakespeare puts into Hamlet's mouth the famous line, "To be or not to be, that is the question," which certain philosophers and literary commentators have interpreted to mean that we either grow and become greater, or we recede and become less. Both spiritual improvement and backsliding can be very subtle and often virtually imperceptible developments in our souls, but one or the other is transpiring in our lives at all times, as apparently the Poet saw. Growth in either virtue or vice will continue in our souls. We should constantly pray that it be virtue. Our Lord tells us, "Pray, lest ye enter into temptation." (*Luke* 22:40). Also, "Take ye heed, watch and pray, for you know not when the time is." (*Mark* 13:33). "And he spoke also a parable to them, that we ought always to pray and not to faint." (*Luke* 18:1). Plus, St. Paul admonishes us to "Pray without ceasing. In all things give thanks, for this is the will of God." (*1 Thessalonians* 5:17-18). The *Treatise* will teach us how to be certain in our own case that it is virtue, not vice, that constantly gains the ground in our souls.

Thus, meditation and prayer are essential to salvation—meditation to keep before our minds the reality of God and His truths, and the prayer of petition to ask for the grace or help from God to save our souls. God created us human beings as rational creatures, and we need correct ideas in our minds to guide our lives; that is where meditation on the eternal truths of our Faith enters the equation, to keep before our mind's eye the realities of True Religion, that we may retain the realization of why we are on earth and what it is we must do to save our souls. For this reason meditation, or mental prayer, is crucially important to our salvation. And that is why *Treatise on Prayer and Meditation*— being the easily read but thorough and authoritative handbook on the subject that it is—in turn is a vital tool to assist us in gaining our salvation and eternal reward.

For this present edition of the *Treatise on Prayer and Meditation,* we have used the Dominic Devas, O.F.M. translation of 1926, previously published by Burns, Oates and Washbourne, that includes also the short work *Pax Animae* of John of Bonilla. Basically, the text is the same as the original translation, save for the following improvements: 1) The copy has been entirely retypeset in a new format; 2) the entire text has been re-edited for correct punctuation and the elimination of a great deal of unnecessary and simply wrong punctuation, especially the overuse of commas, so typical of many older texts; 3) all Bible quotes have been carefully checked for accuracy, and where the exact quote has not been used, a "Cf." has been added before the Bible reference; 4) all Bible quotes and short book references have been shifted from footnotes to references within the text for ease in reading; 5) because the author apparently (but possibly only the translator) used a very "clipped" style of writing, with many words left out that can usually be understood from the context, these "omitted words" have often been included without notation, (being only an improvement of the translation), but sometimes they are added within brackets to facilitate understanding; 6) some rearranging of the word order of sentences has been done where this makes the sentence more readily understood; 7) where the author calls for a series of points to be seriously considered, bracketed numbers have been added and the points italized to highlight them, 8) the footnotes have been re-edited and expanded where necessary and new footnotes added, which latter have "—*Editor,* 2008" added after them; and 9) the Dedication of St. Peter and the Introduction from the 1926 edition have been retained in this edition.

Sometime early in the publishing history of *Treatise on Prayer and Meditation*, the short tract *Pax Animae* was appended to it. For the purposes of this edition, we have decided to leave it in the book. However, a certain *caveat,* or caution, needs to be given the reader who is serious about engaging in mental prayer.

The great handbook on mental prayer is the *Treatise,* not *Pax Animae.* Because this latter is an entirely different book, by a different author and covers the subject from a somewhat different perspective from that of the *Treatise,* reading it immediately after finishing the *Treatise* is likely to neutralize somewhat the advice given by St. Peter in his book and dilute the effect that the *Treatise* should have. Therefore, it is strongly suggested to the reader—if he really wants to put into practice the advice contained in the *Treatise*—that he skip reading *Pax Animae* until a later time. And when he does read it, that he consider it strictly on its own merits and not along with or necessarily connected to the advice given by St. Peter.

These things said, and in conclusion, may this new edition of *Treatise on Prayer and Meditation* achieve for the reader what St. Peter of Alcantara conceived and desired it to achieve: May it bring to its readers a much richer spiritual life and a fuller conception of the beauties and hidden lessons contained in our Holy Religion.

The Publisher
August 20, 2008
St. Bernard

INTRODUCTION

1. The Author

ST. PETER was born in 1499 at Alcantara, a Spanish town practically on the confines of Portugal. Alexander VI was reigning at Rome, and Henry VII in England. Spain itself was mostly subject to the wise rule of Ferdinand and Isabella, and Peter's father was governor of their town of Alcantara. As a boy, Peter followed for two years or so the course of law in the university of Salamanca. When he was sixteen, he joined, though not without an interior struggle, the Order of St. Francis and was clothed in the habit at the convent of Manjarez by Fr. Michael Roco. After his profession, he was sent to Belvis and later to Badajoz. In 1524 he was ordained priest and the following year named Guardian of the convent of Los Angeles at Robredillo.

For thirteen years Peter was actively engaged in all the labors of an apostolic life and in much preaching. In 1538 he was elected Provincial of his Province of St. Gabriel. His favorite residence at this period was the convent of St. Michael at Plasencia, and it was here that he drew up special statutes for the good ordering of his Province. He knew the convent well; it was a novitiate house, and already he had trained novices there.

In 1541, when his term of office had expired, he withdrew into Portugal with Father John of Aguila. Some years back, King John III (and his family) had begged the Saint to visit him, for the fame of his sanctity was widespread; but it was in a lonely region among the mountains of Arabida that Peter settled, lending the powerful influence of his name and example to help establish there *a custody** of austere contemplative Franciscans.

In 1544, he returned to Spain as Definitor of the Province of St. Gabriel, and devoted himself once more to an apostolic life, and very specially to the spread of the Third Order. In 1548, at the chapter held at Alconchel, he successfully withstood the genuine efforts that were made there to choose him again as Provincial, and this done, he returned again to Portugal to consolidate the

* *I.e.,* a small group of friaries, ruled by a *Custos.*

little *custody* he was so interested in, which was suffering somewhat from the death of its chief promotor, Fr. Martin of St. Mary. In this work he was helped by his friend St. Francis Borgia. After three years he came back to Spain; in 1533, he was at the General Chapter of Salamanca, looking like "the living image," as men thought, of his great father St. Francis; then he seems to have withdrawn into complete retirement, and at La Lapa near Badajoz about 1556 to have written his *Tratado de la Oración y Meditación—Treatise on Prayer and Meditation.*

At this period he was busy about his own *reform*. In 1555 he was at Rome securing the requisite authority. In the following year his penitent, the *most devout* Rodrigo de Chaves, to whom the *Tratado* is dedicated, offered him a foundation at Pedroso. Peter accepted it and built up there his *ideal* convent, in the strictest poverty: not even the pathetic appeal of the retired Emperor, Charles V, coupled with that of St. Francis Borgia, could summon him thence to Portugal. The *reform* spread rapidly, by the double process of absorbing old foundations already existing and establishing new ones. By the end of the century it was, I suppose, the dominant Franciscan influence in Spain.

It was in this final period of his life that

Peter came into intimate relations with St. Teresa of Avila. She acknowledges often and in most generous terms all the help he gave her, both individually for her own spiritual guidance, and exteriorly in the great work of rebuilding Carmel to which God had set her.

On October 18, in the year 1562, St. Peter died at Arenas, on his knees, and simultaneously appeared to St. Teresa, telling her "he was going to rest." He was beatified in 1622 and canonized on April 28, 1669.

II. THE BOOK

Apart from some letters, a short writing on St. Teresa and the Constitutions of his reform, the *Tratado de la Oración y Meditación* is the sole work left us by this master of an apostolic and spiritual life.[1] Like a better known work, emanating likewise from sixteenth-century Spain, the *Tratado* might well be styled *The Spiritual Exercises of Saint Peter of Alcantara,* for it is less a book of meditations than a guide to the interior life. Like the *Exercises* of St. Ignatius, it

---

1. The exquisite little treatise, *Pax Animae,* familiar to many in Canon Vaughan's edition and attributed to St. Peter, is really the work of a contemporary Spanish Franciscan, Father John of Bonilla. See *Traité de la Paix de l'Ame* by P. Ubald d'Alençon: de Gigord, Paris, 1912, and *Introduction, infra,* p. 169 of this edition.

begins by suggesting thoughts on the end of man, on death and judgment, on Heaven and Hell, and then passes forward to considerations on the humanity of Jesus Christ and His Passion. Finally, where St. Ignatius has his *Contemplation for Obtaining Love,* St. Peter gives us his *Special Prayer for the Love of God,* a prayer which is uniquely the Saint's own work and found in none of the writings on which he was drawing. It forms the culminating point of the book and is redolent of that true Franciscan spirit of *affective* prayer.

It is also interesting to note the Saint's teaching on contemplation. Needless to say, he sees nothing extravagant in the ordinary person's aiming at it [Fr. Garrigou-Lagrange shares this opinion]; on the contrary, it is the normal term of meditation and *discursive* prayer, which is but the "ladder" leading to contemplation. Meditation is the striking of the flint to secure the spark. "In contemplation, however," writes St. Peter, "the light is already lit—*i.e.,* the sentiment and desired *affection* of the will is already present, and one rests thereon and enjoys it in silence, no longer with much reasoning and speculation of the intellect, but just with undivided atten-

---

2. Part I, Ch. xii, 8th Counsel. See page 112.

tion, gazing upon Truth."[2] Clearly the Saint is here referring to what has been rightly classified as *active* contemplation—a form of prayer to which all may, with God's accompanying grace, aspire. Very different is *passive* contemplation, a special gift of God to certain chosen souls, and not infrequently accompanied by "visions, revelations, ecstasies and so forth," which no one should desire, and "which may be very dangerous indeed to such as are not founded in humility."[3]

Of the actual value of this little book, it will be enough to recall what such Saints as Teresa and Francis de Sales have said. The former, in the thirtieth chapter of *Her Life,* speaks of St. Peter's work on prayer as being "in the hands of almost everyone. And it is not surprising that one who practiced it with so much purity, should have written on it so well and so profitably." St. Francis de Sales, quite briefly, in a letter to the wife of President Brulart, says: "Alcantara is very good for prayer."[4] [St.] John of Avila, the famous apostle of Andalusia, is eloquent in praise of St. Peter, and the Spanish Carthusian of Miraflores, Dom Antony of Molina, recommends to his sister to use the Saint's little

---

3. Part II, Ch. V, 2nd Counsel.
4. *Letters to Persons in the World,* Ed. Mackey, p. 68.

treatise in her study of mental prayer. In his own book, *Exercicios Espirituales,* he quotes with approval the Saint's advice in the matter of spiritual consolations.[5]

II. THE TRANSLATION

It may be said at once that this translation would never have been made if it had not been for the guidance of Fr. Michael Bihl, O.F.M., pointing out where reliable texts were to be found and for the ready kindness of Fr. Ubald d'Alencon, O.S.F.C. in allowing me to make free use of his own excellent French translation of the *Tratado.*[6] Without this, it would have been quite impossible for me to embark on this undertaking, and it has been my main stand-by throughout. I may also add that I have had before me the Spanish text published at Medina del Campo in 1587 and lately reproduced by Fr. Andrew de Ocerin-Jauregui, O.F.M.[7] To this Spanish text I have made continuous reference and have been able, in consequence, to supply here and there a word, or even a few lines, which appear to have been overlooked in the

---

5. *Exercicios Espirituales,* p. 47: Barcelona, 1776.
6. *Traité de l'Oraison et da la Méditation:* Paris, Librairie Saint-François, 1923.
7. *Tratado de la Oración y Meditación:* Madrid, Hijos de Gregorio del Amo, 1919.

French translation. The earliest extant edition of the *Treatise* of St. Peter is apparently one published at Lisbon by John Blavio about 1558.

Contents

PART I

PART II

PAX ANIMAE

Treatise On
Prayer And Meditation

"And these words which I command thee this day shall be in thy heart: And thou shalt tell them to thy children, and thou shalt meditate upon them, sitting in thy house and walking on thy journey, sleeping and rising."

—Deuteronomy 6:6-7

PART I

WHICH TREATS OF MEDITATION

CHAPTER 1

On the Fruit One May Draw from Prayer and Meditation

A S THIS short treatise deals with prayer and meditation, it will be useful to point out in a few words the fruit one may gather from this holy exercise. Thus, with a more joyous heart will men apply themselves to it.

It is well known that one of the greatest obstacles which hinders a man from attaining his supreme happiness and good is the evil inclination of the heart and the difficulty and disinclination experienced in doing what is right. Were it not for this, it would be a very easy thing to run in the path of virtue and to attain the end for which he was created. Hence the Apostle says: "I am delighted with the law of God, according to the inward man; but I see another law in my members, fighting against the law of my mind, and captivating me in the law of sin." (*Romans* 7:22-23). Herein, then, you see the universal cause of all our evil.

To remove this distaste and difficulty and to help us in this affair, one of the most effective instruments is devotion. Devotion, as St. Thomas says (IIa, IIae, q. 82, a.I.), is nothing other than a certain promptitude and facility in well-doing, which banishes from our souls all difficulty and heaviness and makes us prompt and ready to undertake all that is good. It is a spiritual nourishment, a refreshment, a dew from Heaven, a breath wafted to us from the Holy Spirit, a supernatural *affection*. It so regulates, strengthens and transforms the heart of man as to give him a new taste and keenness for spiritual things, and a new distaste and horror for sensual things. Everyday experience shows us that, on emerging from profound and devout prayer, a spiritual person renews in himself all his good resolutions: there it is that he receives favors and steels himself in well-doing; there does he desire to please and love a Lord who has shown Himself so good and so gentle; there does he think of accomplishing fresh labors and of suffering and of shedding his blood for Him; there, finally, does he rejuvenate and renew all the freshness of his soul.

If you ask me how to win this so strong and noble affection for devotion, it is the same holy doctor who replies by saying that it is by means of meditation and contemplation on divine things. This deep meditation and thought does in fact engender that affection and sentiment in the will which we call devotion, and this incites and urges us on to well-doing. Hence, this holy exercise is highly recommended by all the Saints, since it is the means for acquiring devotion. Devotion is in itself a single virtue, but it prepares us and moves us forward to all the other virtues and gives a general impulse to them all. If you would be convinced of this, see how clearly St. Bonaventure puts it in the following words:[1]

"If you would endure with patience the adversities and miseries of this life, be a man of prayer. If you would acquire strength and courage to vanquish the temptations of the enemy, be a man of prayer. If you would crush your self-will, with all its inclinations and desires, be a man of prayer. If you would know the wiles of Satan and defend yourself against his snares, be a man of prayer. If you would live with a joyous heart and pass lightly along the road of penance and sacrifice, be a man of prayer. If you would drive away vain thoughts and cares which worry the soul like flies, be a man of prayer. If you would nourish the soul

---

1. *Meditations on the Life of Christ,* c. 73, a work no longer to be ascribed to St. Bonaventure, but rather to the Franciscan, Joannes a Caulibus. See *Opera Omnia S. Bonaventurae,* t. x of the Quaracchi edition.

with the sap of devotion and have it always
filled with good thoughts and desires, be a
man of prayer. If you would strengthen and
establish your heart in the way[s] of God, be a
man of prayer. Finally, if you would uproot
from your soul all vices and plant virtues in
their place, be a man of prayer. For herein
does a man receive the unction and grace of
the Holy Spirit, who teaches all things. Nay
more, would you mount to the summit of contemplation and enjoy the sweet embraces of
the Spouse, exercise yourself in prayer, for it
is the road that leads to contemplation and to
the taste of what is heavenly. Do you see now
how great is the strength and power of
prayer? In proof of all that has been said—
apart from the witness of the divine Scrip-
tures—let that suffice for the moment as
proof sufficient what we have heard and seen,
what we see every day, viz., many simple persons who have achieved all we have enumer-
ated above, and even greater, by the exercise
of prayer."

Such are the words of St. Bonaventure.
What treasure could one find richer or fuller
than that? Listen again to what another very
religious and holy doctor says on this subject,
speaking of the same virtue.[1]

---

1. St. Lawrence Justinian, *Lignum Vitae: De Oratione,* c. 2.

"In prayer," he says, "the soul cleanses itself from sin, charity is nourished, faith is strengthened, hope is made secure, the spirit rejoices, the soul grows tender, and the heart is purified; truth discovers itself, temptation is overcome, sadness takes to flight, the senses are renewed, failing virtue is made good, tepidity disappears, the rust of sin is rubbed away. In it are brought forth lively flashes of heavenly desires, and in these fires rises the flame of divine love. Great are the excellences of prayer, great its privileges. The heavens open before it and unveil therein their secrets, and to it are the ears of God ever attentive."

Let this suffice to give some idea of the fruit of this holy exercise.

CHAPTER 2

On the Subject Matter of Meditation

Having seen the immense value of prayer and meditation, let us consider now the subjects on which we ought to meditate. As the purpose of this holy exercise is to establish in our hearts the love and the fear of God and fidelity to His Commandments, so the most suitable subject-matter for this exercise will be that which is most adapted to this end. It is of course true that all material things and all that is spiritual and sacred may serve this purpose; still, speaking generally, the mysteries of our Faith as contained in the Creed or *Credo* are the most efficacious and effective, for herein the benefits of God are treated of— the Last Judgment, the pains of Hell and the glory of Heaven—and these act strongly upon our heart and move it to the love and fear of God. It treats also of the Life and Passion of Christ, our Saviour, and herein lies all our good. Here, then, are two groups of subjects especially noted in the *Credo*, and it is mostly around these that we ponder in meditation, so that with good reason is it said that the *Credo* contains the matter most suitable for this holy exercise. This, however, must not be taken to mean that that is not the best for each person which most effectively moves his heart to the love and fear of God.

In order to introduce newcomers and beginners to this path and to provide them with the sustenance which suits them—already prepared and masticated beforehand—I shall give here briefly two sets of meditations for each day of the week, one for the evening and one for the morning, drawn for the most part from the mysteries of our Faith. As we give two repasts a day to our bodies, so do we similarly give two to our souls, whose nourishment lies in meditation on and consideration of divine things. Of these meditations, one set is on the Sacred Passion and Resurrection of Christ; the remainder on the other mysteries mentioned above. He who cannot find the time to recollect himself twice every day can at least devote one week to the first set of mysteries and the second week to the other; or he may confine himself to those [mysteries] on the Life and Passion of Jesus Christ, as these are the more important. It is not wise, however, at the beginning of conversion to neglect the others, for they are very suitable for that period in which most of all is required the fear of God and contrition and hatred of sin.

FIRST SERIES OF MEDITATIONS FOR EVERY DAY OF THE WEEK

Monday

SIN AND SELF-KNOWLEDGE

Today you may occupy yourself with the remembrance of sin and with the knowledge of yourself. The one will show you all the evil there is in you; the other will convince you that you have nothing which is not from God.

This is the way to win humility, the mother of all virtues.

Think, in the first place, of the many sins of your past life, especially of those you committed when you knew less of God. If you consider well, you will find them to be more numerous than the hairs of your head (Cf. *Psalms* 39:13) and that you lived in those days like a pagan who knows not what God is. Go briefly through the Ten Commandments of God and the Seven Capital Sins, and you will find there is not one into which you have not often fallen by action or by word or by thought.

In the second place, think of all the benefits of God and of the different periods of your past life, in what fashion you have used them; for of all must you render an account to God. Tell me how have you spent your childhood, and your adolescence, and your youth, and finally all the days of your past life? How have you used the senses of the body and the powers of the soul, which God has given you that you might know and serve Him? How have you used your eyes, if not to gaze upon vanity? And your ears, if not to listen to falsehood? And your tongue, if not in every fashion of oath and slander? And your taste and smell and touch, if not in pleasures and sensual caresses?

How have you profited by the Holy Sacraments, which God has instituted for a remedy? How have you thanked Him for His benefits? How have you corresponded with His inspirations? How have you utilized your health and energy, your natural talents, your material resources, the facilities and opportunities you have had of leading a good life? What interest have you had in your neighbor, whom God has commended to you, and in those works of mercy He has bid you engage in for His sake? What answer will you give in the Day of Account, when God will say to you: "Give an account of your stewardship, and of the goods entrusted to you, for I no longer wish you to administer them?" (Cf. *Luke* 16:2). O barren tree, all prepared for eternal torments! How will you answer on that day when you must explain all your life and every moment and minute thereof?

In the third place, think of the sins you have committed and commit every day since the time you opened your eyes to the knowledge of God. You will find that the old Adam (Cf. *Romans* 6:6) still lives in you in many an old and deep-rooted habit. See how insolent you have been toward God, how ungrateful for His benefits, how rebellious to His inspirations, how slothful in His service. Never do you do anything for Him with promptitude and diligence, nor with the requisite purity of intention, but other motives and worldly interests move you.

Consider, moreover, how hard you are toward your neighbor and compassionate toward yourself, a lover of your own will, of the flesh, of your honor and of your own interests. See how proud you are and ambitious, hot-tempered, overbearing, vain and envious, full of malice, self-indulgent, inconstant, lacking respect, sensual, intent on your own amusements and conversations, on your laughter and idle words. Mark how inconstant you are in your good resolutions, how inconsiderate in your words, how negligent in your work, how weak and irresolute in every grave affair.

In the fourth place, having considered, in order, the great number of your sins, ponder on their gravity, that you may gauge every aspect of your wretchedness. To this end, you ought first to consider these three circumstances of the sins of your past life, namely: *Against whom* you have sinned; *Why* you have sinned; and *In what way* you have sinned. If you look *against whom* you have sinned, you will see that you have sinned against God, whose kindness and majesty are infinite, whose benefits to man and whose mercies are more numerous than the sands of the sea. And *why* have you sinned? For a point of honor, for some bestial pleasure, for some tiny interest, and often for nothing at all, but just from custom and depreciation of God. *In what manner* have you sinned? With such ease, such boldness, so unscrupulously, so fearlessly, nay, at times, with such readiness and content as if you were sinning against a god of wood, knowing and seeing nothing of what passes in the world. Is this the honor due to so great a Majesty? Is this the gratitude for such great benefits? Is this the price of that Precious Blood shed on the Cross, of those blows and buffets received for you? Wretched [are you] in what you have lost, still more so in what you have done, and most of all if you do not recognize your sorry plight.

After this, it will be very useful to fix the eyes of your mind on the study of your own nothingness. Of yourself, you hold nothing at all except sin; all the rest comes from God. It is clear that the gifts of Nature and those of grace (which are the greater) are wholly His; to Him belongs the grace of predestination (which is the source of all the other graces), to Him the grace of vocation, to Him concomitant grace [that assists us all the while we are performing a good action], to Him the grace of perseverance, to Him the grace of eternal life. What have you then in which to glory but your nothingness and sin? Rest awhile in the consideration of this nothingness—for this is all you have, the remainder is all God's—that thus you may see plainly and distinctly what you are and what He is, your poverty and His riches, and how little, in consequence, you should trust in yourself and esteem yourself, and how much you should trust in Him and love Him and glorify yourself in Him.

Thinking then over all these points I have mentioned, have of yourself the very lowest esteem possible. Consider yourself as nothing better than a wild reed which bends before every wind, without weight or strength or firmness, unstable and with no sort of solidity. Consider yourself as Lazarus, four days in the tomb, a corpse tainted and horrible, full of worms, so that every passerby holds his nose and closes his eyes before such a sight. Imagine that it is thus you appear to God and His Angels; hold yourself unworthy to lift your eyes toward Heaven, unworthy of the earth that bears you, of the creatures that serve you, of the very bread you eat and the air you breathe. Cast yourself at the feet of the Saviour with her who was a public sinner (Cf. *Luke* 7:37-50); cover yourself with the shame of a woman before her husband whose honor she has betrayed; with great sorrow and repentance of heart ask forgiveness for your wanderings and that, of His infinite goodness and mercy, He may deign to receive you back into His house.

Tuesday

ON THE MISERIES OF THIS LIFE

Today you will meditate upon the miseries of human life. Thus you will see how vain is the glory of the world, how fit to be despised, for it has no other frail foundation than this miserable life. The defects and miseries of this life are, as it were, innumerable. You may consider especially the seven following:

Consider *first* that this life is short, some seventy or eighty years at most, and if it stretches beyond, is, as the Prophet says, *"but labor and sorrow."* (*Psalm* 89:10). Take from this the period of infancy, which is more an animal than a human life, and the time spent in sleep, during which we neither use our senses nor that reason of ours which is proper to man, and you will see that life is even shorter than at first appears. If, moreover, you compare it with the eternity of the life to come, it will seem to you hardly a speck. Thus you will perceive how infatuated those are who, to enjoy so short a breath of life, expose themselves to lose the repose of that which is to last forever.

Secondly, consider how uncertain this life is. Here is another misery to add to the former, for as though it were not enough that it is so short, it is also without security and is uncertain. How many reach those seventy or eighty years I mentioned? For how many are the strands broken when they would begin to weave! How many pass away in the flower of their age, as we put it, or before they reach maturity! "You know not," as the Saviour says, "at what hour your Lord will come," (Cf. *Mark* 13:35), in the morning or at midday, at midnight or at the cock-crowing. Better to appreciate this truth, think of the deaths of the many persons you have known in this world, especially of your friends and comrades, and of persons who have been famous and admired. At varying ages in life has death struck them and swept away all their schemes and hopes.

Thirdly, consider how frail and delicate this life is, and you will see that no vessel of glass is so fragile. A breeze or a hot sun, a draught of cold water or the breath of a sick person—these are enough to despoil us of it, as everyday experience shows. How many a man is cut down in the flower of his age from one or other of these causes.

In the *fourth* place, see how mutable this life is, never the same for long. Think how our bodies change; they do not remain permanently in the one same regular state of health; much less do our souls. Like the sea, these are always restless under the varying winds and waves of passion, of craving, of desire, which trouble us at every hour. Think, finally, of the changes of fortune: no one willingly consents to remain in the same state of life, with the same measure of prosperity, the same joy, but human life is like a wheel, forever rolling on. Above all, dwell on the unceasing movement of life: day or night, it never pauses, lessening as it moves. What is our life but a torch that is forever consuming itself? The more resplendently it burns, the more rapidly will it fail. What is our life but a flower, which opens out in the morning and blooms at midday, and in the evening withers? (Cf. *Job* 14:2). It is by reason of this continuous change that God says by the mouth of Isaias, "All flesh is grass, and all the glory thereof as the flower of the field." (*Isaias* 40:6). St. Jerome (In Cap. 40, *Isaias*) comments thus upon these words: "Truly, when we consider the frailty of our flesh and how at every point and moment of time we increase and decrease, without ever remaining in the same state, and how that which at this very instant forms the subject of

our discourse, of our schemes and meditations, is to such an extent cut off from our life,
we shall not hesitate to speak of our flesh as a
little grass and all its glory as the flower of
the field." The infant at the breast, how
quickly does it grow into a child, and the child
into a big lad, and lo and behold, the big lad is
soon well on in years, and when on the verge
of old age, marvels to find himself no longer
young! The woman whose beauty attracted
the attention of so many young men soon
finds herself with wrinkled brow, and she who
was once so attractive quickly becomes an
object of aversion.

Fifthly, consider how deceitful life is. This
is perhaps the worst feature of all, so many
does she lead astray; so many cling to her in
blind affection. She is ugly, and we fancy her
beautiful; bitter, and she appears to us sweet;
short, and each one esteems her enduring;
she seems spacious, and is narrow; she seems
so lovable that there is no peril nor labor men
will not face for her, even at the risk of life
eternal, doing such things as lead them to the
loss of the life which knows no end.

Sixthly, consider how this life, already burdened with those miseries we have mentioned, is subject also to so many misfortunes
both of soul and body. Nothing else is it than
a valley of tears and a sea of measureless

sorrow. St. Jerome relates how Xerxes, that mighty monarch who levelled out the mountains and filled in the seas, found himself one day looking down from an eminence upon a countless host of armed men. He admired them for some time and then began to weep. Questioned on the cause of his tears, he replied: "I weep because a hundred years hence not one of those I see before me will be alive." "Would that we," adds St. Jerome, "could mount to some such height from which we might view all the world at our feet. Then might we see the falls and disasters of all the world: nations destroyed one by the other, and kingdom by kingdom. Here would we see torments, and in another place massacre; some perishing at sea, others led away captive; here a wedding, there a death; some dying by violence, others in peace; some abounding in wealth, others in beggary. Finally, we should see not merely the army of Xerxes, but all men in the world living today, and doomed in a few days to vanish." (*Funeral Oration on Nepotian*).

Think of all the infirmities and labors of man's body, all the afflictions and anxieties of his soul, all the perils that accompany man in every state and in every period of his life, and you will see well enough the miseries of human life, and clearly too how little the world can give. Thus will you easily come to hold in little esteem all that there is in it.

To all these miseries succeeds *the last,* which is death. For body and soul alike, this is the final terror. In an instant the body is stripped of all, and the soul fixed forever in its eternity.

This meditation will help to make you understand how short and wretched is the glory of the world—yet it is on this that a worldly life relies—and consequently, how reasonable it is to disdain and to scorn it.

Wednesday

ON DEATH

Today you will think of that passing away which we call death. This is one of the most useful considerations for acquiring true wisdom and for avoiding sin, as well as for leading us to prepare in time for the hour of judgment.

Consider in the first place how uncertain is the moment in which death will lay you low. You know neither the day, nor the place, nor in what state you will be when it comes. You know only that you must die; all the rest is uncertain, except this, that ordinarily it comes when a man is least desirous of it and thinking least about it.

Secondly, consider the parting it occasions, not merely from the things we have loved in this life, but even between soul and body, so long such close partners. To be banished from one's country and no longer able to breathe one's native air is looked on as a great evil, even though the exile carry with him all he loves. How much harder, then, will that exile be which is total, withdrawing us from all that is in our house, from our possessions, from our friends, from our father and mother and sons, from air and light, and indeed from all things! The bull lows when separated from its mate with which it worked. What will not be the cry of your heart when you are separated from the company of all those who help you in bearing the burdened yoke of life?

Consider again the distress a man experiences when he calls to mind the fate which awaits his soul and his body after death. For his body, he knows that nothing better is in store than a seven-foot grave, side by side with the other dead; for the soul, nothing sure, neither as to its future nor as to its fate. Herein lies an anguish none greater than which one can suffer. We know of glory and of unending pain; we are on the brink of the one or the other, yet we are ignorant as to which of these two so unequal destinies awaits us. (Cf. *Ecclesiastes* 9:12).

To this yet another, and no less an anguish succeeds: the account that we must render; even the most valiant tremble before this. It is related of the monk Arsenius that, when on the point of death, he began to tremble. "Father," said his disciples, "are you afraid now?" "My children," he answered, "it is no new thing in me, this fear; I have had it always." (*Life* by Rufinus, Bk. 3). At this moment, in fact, a man pictures all his sins as a squadron of hostile cavalry charging down upon him, and the greater sins—those in which he reveled the deeper—stand out conspicuous above the rest and terrify him the more. Oh how bitter now is the memory of those past delights, which at the time seemed so sweet! Well does the wise man say: "Look not upon the wine when it is yellow, when the colour thereof shineth in the glass. It goeth in pleasantly, but in the end, it will bite like a snake and will spread abroad poison like a basilik." (*Proverbs* 23:31-32). These are the poisoned dregs of the drink the enemy proffers us; this is the bitter aftertaste from the gilded chalice of Babylon.

Surrounded by so many accusers, a man thus wretched begins to fear the terror of this Judgment. "Miserable that I am," he says within himself, "to have lived in error and walked by such paths as these; what will become of me in this Judgment?" St. Paul tells us that "What things a man shall sow, those also shall he reap." (*Galatians* 6:8). And what have I sown, if not the works of the flesh; what can I look for, then, but corruption? St. John says that in the Heavenly City all is pure gold and that nothing defiled shall enter in; (Cf. *Apocalypse* 21:21, 27). What then can he hope for who has lived a life so evil and so shameful?

There come now the Sacraments of Confession and Communion, and of Extreme Unction, last succors which the Church brings to us to help us in these terrible moments. See here again the anxiety and anguish suffered by the man who has led an evil life, how he wishes now that he had followed another course, how different a life would he lead henceforward were time allowed him. He will indeed appeal to God, yet the pain and grip of disease will but hardly allow such recourse.

Note also the final accompaniments of the malady which herald the approach of death; how terrible they are and awe-inspiring: the heaving chest, the hoarse voice. The feet lose all sense of touch, the knees grow icy cold, the nose runs, the eyes sink in, the face is deathly white, the tongue can function no longer, and finally the soul battles to depart, and all the tormented senses lose their power and strength. But above all, it is the soul that suffers most; in agony she struggles, fearing to go, dreading the Judgment that is being prepared. She has no natural desire for this separation; she clings lovingly to her state; she fears the Tribunal of Justice.

At length the soul leaves the body; and now two courses are open to you: by one, you may accompany the body to the tomb; by the other, follow the soul and witness the final fixing of its fate. Consider what happens in both cases. Think of the body after the soul has left it. Rich apparel is produced in which to clothe it for burial, and then all possible speed is made to remove it from the house. Consider all the details of the burial, the tolling bells, the questions men ask each other about the dead, the service in the church with its mournful music, the funeral procession and the weeping friends—in fact, all the circumstances that usually accompany the laying of a body in the tomb, the land of perpetual oblivion.

This done, turn to the soul and watch the road she takes toward those unknown regions, the place where she ultimately halts and the Judgment that follows. Imagine yourself present at this Judgment and that the whole Court of Heaven is waiting there to hear the final sentence. Questions will be asked and answers given for everything that you have received, down to the very point of a needle. There must account be rendered for the gift of life and worldly goods and family, for the inspirations of God and for all that might have helped you on to a holy life, and above all, for the blood of Christ. And according to the account each one will render, so will he be judged.

Thursday

THE LAST JUDGMENT

Today you will think of the Last Judgment. This consideration will foster in your soul those two important sentiments which should animate every faithful Christian, viz., fear of God and hatred of sin.

Consider in the first place, how terrible that day will be on which will be tried the case of every child of Adam, on which our own cases will be settled and the final sentence as to our future published. That day will gather to itself the days of every century—past, present and to come. Then shall the world render account of its ages; then shall the anger of God—pent up throughout the centuries—break forth. How impetuously will this river of divine indignation burst out, receiving as many affluent streams of wrath and anger as there have been sins committed from the beginning of the world.

Secondly, mark the dreadful signs heralding that day. Before that day shall come, as the Saviour says, "There shall be signs in the sun and in the moon and in the stars," (*Luke* 21:25), and in short, among all creatures in Heaven and on earth. Before it is yet upon them, all will feel the end approaching and in great distress will begin to tremble before they fall. "Men," He adds, will shrink up and "wither away for fear," (Cf. *Luke* 21:26), as they listen to the dreadful roaring of the sea and watch the great waves and the raging tempest, terrible indications portending the awful calamities and miseries predicted for the world. They will wander about, stupefied and amazed, pallid and haggard, as men dead before death has reached them, as men judged before the sentence has been proclaimed, measuring their peril by their own fears, each one so busy over himself as to be heedless of his neighbor, even the father heedless of his child. None can serve his fellow, and yet none can stand alone.

Thirdly, contemplate that universal deluge of fire which is to precede the coming of the Judge; hearken to the challenging notes of the archangel's trumpet, summoning to one place all the generations of the world to be present at the Judgment; see the awe-inspiring majesty of the approaching Judge.

Turn now to the thought of the rigid severity of the account each one must render. Truly, as Job says, "Man cannot be justified compared with God. If he will contend with him, he cannot answer him one for a thousand." (*Job* 9:2-3). What will the wicked feel when God examines each one, saying to him in the interior of his conscience: "Come hither, thou evil man, what hast thou seen in Me to despise Me thus, and to pass into the camp of My enemy? To My own image and likeness have I created thee; I have given to thee the light of faith; I have made a Christian of thee; with My own blood have I ransomed thee. It was for thee I fasted and journeyed, watched and toiled; for thee My sweat became as drops of blood; for thee I suffered persecution and blows, blasphemy and derision, mockery, dishonor, torments—and at last, the Cross. See here the Cross and the nails; see still upon My body the wounds of feet and hands; before this sky and earth I suffered, and they bear witness still. What hast thou done with that soul of thine which I, by My blood, made Mine? At what work hast thou employed what I so dearly won? O foolish and adulterous generation! Why hast thou rather sought in weariness to serve

thine enemy, than in joy to serve Me, thy
Redeemer and Creator? So often have I called
thee, and thou didst not answer; I have
knocked upon thy door, and thou didst not
rouse thyself; I have stretched out My hands
upon the Cross, and thou didst not regard;
thou hast despised My counsels and all My
promises and threats. It is for you now,
Angels of Mine, to speak. Judge, ye judges,
between Me and My vine. What is there that
I ought to have done for it which I have not
done?" (Cf. *Isaias* 5:4).

What reply shall the wicked give, those
who have made a mockery of divine things,
who have ridiculed holiness, who have
despised simplicity, who have preferred the
laws of the world to those of God, men deaf
to every voice of God, insensible to every
inspiration, rebellious against His Commandments, hard and ungrateful before chastise-
ments and benefits alike? How shall they
make answer who have lived as though they
had no belief in God and knew no other law
than that of their own interest? "What will
you do," says Isaias, "in the day of visitation,
and of the calamity which cometh from afar?"
(*Isaias* 10:3). From whom will you seek help,
and of what value to you now will be the
abundance of your wealth?

And now, fifthly, consider the terrible sentence which the Judge will deliver upon the wicked and the awful words which long will linger in the ears of all who hear them. "His lips," as Isaias says, "are filled with indignation, and his tongue as a devouring fire." (*Isaias* 30:27). What fire will leap to flame like these words: "Depart from me, you cursed, into everlasting fire which was prepared for the devil and his angels?" (*Matthew* 25:41). What depth of thought and meaning beneath each single word! Separation, malediction, fire, the company, and above all, the eternity.

Friday

THE PAINS OF HELL

Today you will meditate upon the pains of Hell. This meditation will confirm your soul the more in the fear of God and in horror of sin.

These pains, St. Bonaventure tells us, should be considered under those material aspects and figures such as the Saints have taught us. Thus it is well, he tells us, to imagine the place of Hell as a subterranean lake, dark and obscure, or as a very deep well full of flames, or as a black and terrible city consumed by raging fires, re-echoing to the cries and groans of tormentors and tormented alike, with endless weeping and gnashing of teeth.

This dreadful abode gives rise to two principal kinds of pain: that which is called the pain of *sense* and also the pain of *loss*. As for the former, reflect how there is no exterior nor interior sense that will not have its own proper pain. The wicked have indeed offended God with all their members and all their senses and have made of everything an instrument of sin. Thus will it be ordained that each one [of these will] suffer its proper torment and pay its debt. Here the eyes of adultery and evil living shall endure the awful vision of devils. There the ears that have hearkened to lying and obscenity will listen to unending blasphemy and groans. Here the sense of smell, which has reveled in the scents and sensual odors of vice, will be filled with an intolerable stench. There the taste, which has regaled itself in gluttony and varied dishes, will be tormented with a devouring hunger and with thirst. Here the tongue which has been addicted to murmuring and blasphemy shall feel a bitterness as of the venom of dragons. There the touch, which has lingered lovingly in sweet caressing blandishments, will wade, as Job says, mid the icy waters of the river Cocytus. (Cf. *Job* 21:33; 24:19). Here the imagination will be racked by the apprehension of the present sufferings, the memory by the recollection of past pleasures, the understanding by the thought of future ills, and the will by the immensity of anger and rage which the wicked will entertain against God. There, finally, will be gathered up in one all the evils and torments imaginable. "There will be a cold," says St. Gregory, (*Moralia,* lib. ix, c. 46), "past all endurance, an unquenchable fire, the worm that dieth not, an intolerable odor, darkness that is palpable, the fierce blows of the tormentors, the sight of devils, the disorder of sin, and the despair at seeing the loss of all that is good."

Tell me now, if it is already so insupportably hard to endure even the least of these evils and for the very shortest space of time, what will it be to suffer at one and the same moment, and in all one's members and senses, both interior and exterior, all this multitude of evils, and that, not for the space of one night or a thousand, but throughout an infinite eternity? By what sense or words or judgment can we in this world grasp or fathom this reality?

However, this is not the greatest of the pains therein endured. Greater beyond all comparison is that which theologians call the *pain of loss*. This consists in being forever deprived of the vision of God and of His glorious presence. Now, just as any pain is the greater in proportion to the greatness of the good of which it deprives a man, so also, as God is the Greatest Good of all, the loss of Him will be the greatest evil that there can possibly be.

Such are the pains which all of the damned suffer in general, but besides these general torments, there are the particular ones, which each one individually suffers according to the nature of his sin. There will be a special torment for the proud, for the envious, for the avaricious, for the impure, and so on for the rest. The pain will be commensurate with the sin committed, the shame with the proud presumption of the past, the nakedness with the superabounding excess, the hunger and thirst with the gluttonous pleasures of other days.

With all these torments is coupled that *eternity of suffering* which serves as the seal and lock upon them all. Everything, in fact, may be endured which has an end; for nothing that is transient is really great; but a pain that is endless, without alleviation, decline or diminution, without any prospect of ever ceasing to continue—neither the torment itself, nor the one who inflicts it, nor he who suffers it, a veritable banishment, a clinging garment which may never be laid aside—this indeed breaks the spirit of anyone who attentively considers it.

This is in fact the greatest of all the sufferings endured. For if some limit might be set to the endurance of these afflictions—a thousand years, or a hundred thousand years—or if, as one of the Doctors of the Church puts it, "they hoped to see the end, after having drunk all the waters of the ocean by taking a single drop every thousand years, this would be to them a source of unending consolation." [1] But it is not so; these pains will last with the eternity of God. The duration of these miseries will be measured by that of the divine glory. As long as God shall live, so long shall death endure. When God ceases to be that which He is, then shall the damned cease to be what they are.

Upon this unending eternity of duration, I beg you, Dear Brother of mine, cast your eyes and reflect. Ponder within yourself quite frankly upon these truths. In His Gospel the Eternal Truth speaks to us: "Heaven and earth shall pass, but my words shall not pass." (*Matthew* 24:35).[2]

---

1. *Cf.* St. Gregory, *Moralia,* lib. ix, c. 9.
2. See also *The Exercises of St. Ignatius:* The Fifth Exercise: on Hell.

Saturday

ON HEAVEN

Today you will consider the glory of the Blessed, that thus your heart may be moved to the contempt of the world and to a desire for their company. That you may gather some idea of their felicity, think of these five features of Heaven, viz., the excellence of the place, the happiness of those who are there, the vision of God, the glory of the body, and finally, the complete gathering together there of every good thing.

First, see *the excellence of the place,* and particularly its magnificent spaciousness. We have seen in competent authors that each one of the stars is greater than the earth, some indeed so immense as to be ninety times larger. Looking up into the heavens, we see there a veritable multitude of stars thrown across the empty spaces, from which a whole infinity of things might come down to us. How shall we not stand astonished and abashed at seeing the immensity of Heaven and, what is greater still, that of the Sovereign Lord who made it?

As for *its beauty,* no words can express it. In this valley of tears, in this place of exile, God has created objects admirable and of great beauty. What has He not fashioned, then, in that place wherein His glory dwells, the throne of His greatness, the palace of His Majesty, the home of His thoughts and the paradise of all His delights?

After the excellence of the place, consider *the nobleness of its inhabitants,* their number, their sanctity, their riches and their unimaginable beauty. St. John says that the multitude of the elect is so great that none may count them. (*Apocalypse* 5:11). St. Denis says that the number of the Angels is so great that it surpasses, beyond compare, that of all material things on the earth. (Cf. *De Coelesti Hierarchia,* c. xiv). St. Thomas, following this opinion, teaches that the extent of Heaven is greater, beyond all proportion, than that of the earth and that the multitude of heavenly spirits similarly exceeds that of all material things in the world. (Ia, q. 50, a. 3).

What can one conceive more admirable? Well weighed, this of itself should suffice to astonish all men.

Moreover, each one of these blessed spirits—even the least among them—is more beautiful than all this visible world. What will it be, then, to see such numbers of magnificent beings like this, to gaze upon the perfections and offices of each one of them? The Angels are the messengers of God; the Archangels, ministering spirits; the Powers, triumphal leaders; the Virtues are all resplendent in glory; the Thrones blaze out in light; the Cherubim shine in brilliance and the Seraphim are all aglow; and all sing together the canticles of God. If the mere presence and interchange of all this good have such charm and sweetness, what will it be like to be present there among so many happy ones, to speak with the Apostles, converse with the Prophets and hold intercourse with the Martyrs and all the Elect?

Where there is so much glory in rejoicing in *the company of the good,* what will there be in rejoicing in the company and in the presence of Him whom the stars of the morning praise, whose beauty sun and moon admire, before whose ineffable qualities the Angels and all the heavenly spirits fall prostrate? What will it be to behold this all-comprehensive Good, in whom all that is good in the world resides; nay more, in whom *is* every world; who, though *One,* yet carries all things; though *Simple,* yet includes within Himself all perfections? If it was so wonderful a thing to see and hear Solomon the King, so that the Queen of Saba exclaimed, "Blessed are they who live in your presence and rejoice in your wisdom," (Cf. *3 Kings* 10:8), what will it be to behold this Supreme Solomon, this Eternal Wisdom, this Infinite

Greatness, this Inestimable Beauty, this Immense Goodness, and to rejoice therein forever? Here, then, is the essential glory of the Saints, our Last End and the Harbor of all our Desires.

Pass on now to consider the nature of *the glorified body.* Each will enjoy four special qualities: *subtlety, agility, impassibility* and *clarity,* and the last named will be so great that each one will shine like the sun in the kingdom of the Father. (Cf. *Matthew* 13:43). If a single sun, set in the midst of the heavens, suffices to give light and joy to all this world, what will be the effect of so many suns, of so many resplendent bearers of light?

And now, what can one say of *all the other blessings of Heaven?* There will be health and no sickness, liberty and no servitude, beauty and no unsightliness, immortality and no decay, abundance and no want, repose and no cares, security and no dread, knowledge and no error, satiety and no feelings of revulsion, joy and no sorrow, honor and no contention. "There," says St. Augustine, (Cf. *The City of God,* l. 22. c. 30), "will be true glory, and none will be praised through error or in flattery. There will be true honor, which will not be withheld from the worthy nor conceded to one unworthy. There will be true peace, and none will have anything to suffer, from himself or from others. The reward of virtue will be He who is the Source of virtue and promises Himself as its Reward. One will see Him forever, love Him forever, without wearying, and praise Him without fatigue. There, a resting place, spacious, beautiful, resplendent and sure; a companionship sweet and agreeable; an even tenor of time, without evening or morning, but continuous in an indivisible eternity. It will be as a perpetual summer there, freshened with the undying breath of the Holy Spirit. All are full of joy; all sing about and praise this Sovereign Benefactor, through whose bounty they live and reign eternally. O heavenly city, secure abode, land of delight; O happy citizens, without anything of grief; tranquilly dwelling there, true men, but now at last unburdened. Ah, would that my combat were ended, the days of my exile done! When shall I go and stand before the face of my God?

Sunday

THE BENEFITS OF GOD

Consider today the benefits of God. Render thanks for them to the Lord, and enkindle in yourself a deeper love for One who is so good to you. These benefits are innumerable, but you may at least consider the five principle ones—viz., creation, conservation, redemption, vocation, and finally, all personal and hidden favors.

First is the benefit of *creation*: Consider very attentively what you were before being created, what God has done for you, what He has given you prior to any merit on your part—namely, this body with all its members and senses; this soul so excellent, with its three notable faculties: the understanding, the memory and the will. Note well that in giving you this soul, all else is given you [besides], for there is no perfection at all in any creature which man, in his own measure, does not possess. To give us then this single gift was at the same time to bestow everything else on us as well.

As for the benefit of *conservation*, see how utterly your whole being depends upon the providence of God. Not one instant would you live, not one step would you move, were it not for Him. Everything in the world He has created for your service: sea and land, birds and fishes and animals, the plants and even the very Angels in Heaven. See how He has given you health and strength, life and nourishment, and all other temporal assistance. Above all, think seriously of the miseries and disasters daily befalling other men, into which you also might easily fall, if God in His bounty did not preserve you.

As for the benefit of *redemption*, consider these two points: firstly, the number and grandeur of the benefits He has given us by the grace of Redemption, and secondly, the number and greatness of the woes He suffered in His body and in His most holy soul in order to secure these blessings. In order to appreciate better what you owe to the Lord for all that He has suffered for you, consider these four principal points in the mystery of His Sacred Passion, namely: Who it is that suffers, what He suffers, for whom and why He suffers.

Who suffers? God. What does He suffer? The greatest torments and dishonor that any have ever endured. For whom does He suffer? For creatures, depraved, abominable and, by their actions, like to the very devils themselves. Why does He suffer? Not for His own advantage, nor for any merit in us, but on account of the depth of His own infinite love and mercy.

As for the benefit of *vocation*, consider in the first place how great was the bounty of God in making you a Christian, in calling you through Baptism to the Faith, and allowing you to participate in the other Sacraments. And if despite this call you have lost your innocence, it is He who has drawn you out from sin, re-established you in grace, and set you anew on the path of salvation. How can you praise Him enough for this kindness? How great has been His mercy in thus guarding you so long, in putting up with so many sins, in giving you so many inspirations, instead of cutting short the thread of life, as He does for others in the same state. How mighty has been His grace in raising you from death to life and in opening your eyes to the light; and after your conversion, how great has been His mercy in giving you the grace to sink to sin no more, to overcome the enemy and to persevere in good.

So much for the benefits open and recognized. Besides these, there are others, secret ones, known only to Him who has received them, and some indeed so hidden that even the recipient does not know them, but only He who bestows them. How many times in this life, by your pride or negligence or ingratitude, have you not deserved that God should abandon you, as He would have done to many another such, and yet He has not done so. From how many sins and occasions of sin has not the Lord, in His providence, preserved you by destroying the nets of the enemy, breaking up the way and bringing to nothing his schemes and devices. How often has He not treated us as He did St. Peter, saying, "Behold, Satan hath earnestly desired to have you, that he may sift you all as wheat, but I have prayed for thee, that thy faith fail not." (Cf. *Luke* 22:31-32). Who but God alone knows these secrets? Man may at times recognize the positive benefits of God, but the negative ones—which consist not in bestowing favors upon us, but in delivering us from evils—who shall recognize such as these? For these, as well as for the others, it is right that we should always render thanks to the Lord. We should recognize ourselves as insolvent, so much does the total of our debts surpass that of our means of repayment as to be beyond all reckoning.

CHAPTER 3

On the Fitting Time for and on the Value of these Meditations

Here, then, Dear Reader, are the first seven meditations on which you may philosophize and with which you may occupy your mind each day of the week—not that you may not think on other subjects and set aside certain days on which to do so. For as we have said already, whatever subject leads our hearts to the love and to the fear of God and to the keeping of His Commandments, that is fitting matter for meditation. However, it was necessary, as we have done, to draw out these subjects a little because, on the one hand, they embody the principal mysteries of our Faith, which of their own nature are calculated to lead us on to good, and on the other hand, because beginners, who have need of milk, (Cf. *1 Corinthians* 3:2), will find here, all made ready and prepared for them, the subjects on which they are to meditate. Thus, there is no need for them to grope their way forward like pilgrims in a strange country, nor to hesitate in their movements, taking up one subject, rejecting another, and so on, without ever fixing themselves on any.

We should remember also that these meditations are, as has been said, very suitable at the beginning of conversion, when a man once more returns to God. It is fitting, then, to begin with these subjects, which move us to contrition and to a horror of sin, to the fear of God and to contempt of the world, which are all first steps on the path of virtue. And beginners ought to persevere some little time in the consideration of these subjects, in order thus to establish themselves in holiness and in the virtues named above.

CHAPTER 4

Seven Meditations on the Sacred Passion and the Method To be Employed

Here now are the seven meditations on the holy Passion, Resurrection and Ascension of Christ, to which one may add more on the other principal circumstances of His most holy life.

We should note that, in the Passion of Christ, there are six points to consider: The greatness of His sufferings, that we may compassionate them; the gravity of our sin, which caused them, that we may detest it; the immensity of the benefit, that we may be grateful; the excellence of the divine bounty and love, which shine forth therein, that we too may render love in return; the fittingness of the mystery, that we may admire it; the many virtues of Christ, resplendent here, that we may imitate them.

Conformably to this, we should, as we meditate, incline our heart to compassion for the sorrows of Christ, which were the greatest in the world on account of the delicateness of His body, the greatness of His love, and the fact that they were endured without any kind of consolation, as has been said elsewhere. Or again, we may draw therefrom motives of sorrow for our own sins, seeing that they were the cause of the many and great sufferings He endured; or again, we may find herein motives of love and gratitude, considering the immensity of the love which He shows us and the grandeur of the gift He has given us in redeeming us so fully at such cost to Himself and such profit for ourselves. Or again, we may lift up our eyes and consider the fittingness of the means which God has chosen to heal our wretchedness, to satisfy for our debts, to succor our needs, to enable us to win His grace, to humble our pride, to lead us on to contempt for the world [and] to a love of the Cross, of poverty, of austerity, of injuries and of every other virtuous and fitting act.

Yet again, we may turn our attention to the splendid examples of holiness He has left us in His most sacred life and death: His meekness and patience, His obedience and mercy, His poverty and penance, His charity, humility, kindness and modesty, and all the other virtues which shine forth in His actions and words more brilliantly than the stars of Heaven. Let us imitate a little what we thus see in Him, that the spirit and grace we have received from Him may not find us idle; and thus, through Him, shall we come to Him. Here is indeed the highest and most useful way of meditating on the Passion of Christ, the way, namely, of imitation, for such imitation gradually transforms us, so that we may come to say with the Apostle: "I live, now not I, but Christ liveth in me." (*Galatians* 2:20).

It is fitting, moreover, in all these mysteries to consider Christ as present before our eyes and ourselves as there with Him in His sufferings, and not merely to think of the history of the Passion as a whole, but all the circumstances of it, and especially the four following: *Who* is suffering; *for whom* He suffers; *how* He suffers; and for *what reason*. *Who* suffers? God, all-powerful, infinite, immense. *For whom* does He suffer? For the most ungrateful and thankless creature in the world. *How* does He suffer? With a very great humility and love, kindness and meekness, with mercy, patience and mildness. For *what reason* does He suffer? Not for any interest of His own nor worthiness on our part, but on account of the depths of His infinite pity and mercy.

Finally, let no one content himself with considering the exterior sufferings of Christ, but rather and much more deeply should he ponder on the interior ones. We should fix our attention far more on the soul than on the body of Christ, in order to appreciate His sorrows, His intimate feelings and His thoughts.

After this little introduction, let us begin to take up again and give in order the mysteries of His Sacred Passion.

SEVEN MEDITATIONS ON THE SACRED PASSION

Monday

THE WASHING OF THE FEET AND THE INSTITUTION OF THE BLESSED SACRAMENT

Today, after having made the Sign of the Cross and the usual preparation, let us consider the washing of the feet and the institution of the Most Blessed Sacrament.

Consider, O My Soul, in this scene the gentle and kind Jesus: See the wonderful example of humility He gives you in rising up from the table and washing the feet of His disciples. O good Jesus, what is this You are about? O gentle Jesus, why do You thus humiliate Your Majesty so deeply? My Soul, what feelings would have been yours in seeing Jesus kneeling at the feet of these men, at the feet of Judas? How hard you are, that your heart is not moved in the face of such great humility! How does it come that such great meekness does not rend your heart? Can it be that you have made up your mind to

barter away this Gentle Lamb? Is it possible
that, even with this example before you, you
still have no feelings of compassion? White
and Beautiful Hands, how can you touch
these feet soiled and repulsive? Most Pure
Hands, how does it come that you do not
shrink with horror from washing these feet
covered with the filth of the roads and stained
with blood? O Blessed Apostles, do you not
tremble before such a manifestation of humility? Peter, what are you about? Are you by
chance going to allow the Lord of Majesty to
wash your feet? Quite taken aback and astonished at seeing his Lord prostrate before him,
St. Peter exclaims (Cf. *John* 13:6, 8): "Lord,
dost Thou wash my feet! Art Thou not the Son
of the Living God? Art Thou not the Creator
of the world, the Beauty of Heaven, the Paradise of the Angels, the Saving Hope of men,
the Splendor of the Father's glory, the Source
of the wisdom of God in highest Heaven? And
yet Thou wouldst seek to wash my feet! Thou,
the Lord of such great majesty and glory, dost
Thou wish to fulfill a task so lowly?"

Consider also how, as He finished washing
the feet, He wipes them with the holy towel
with which He is girded. With the eyes of the
soul you may see there an image of the Mystery of our Redemption. See how with the
linen cloth He wipes away all the dirt from

these soiled feet; they become clean, and the linen all stained and soiled with the work. What more sullied than man conceived in sin, and what purer and more beautiful than Christ conceived of the Holy Ghost? "My beloved is white and ruddy," says the Spouse, "chosen out of thousands." (*Canticle of Canticles* 5:10). It is He, so beautiful and so pure, who wills to take upon Himself the stains and filth of our souls; He leaves them clean and free from it all, but with it all, He Himself appears on the Cross shattered and disfigured.

Finally, consider the words with which the Saviour concludes this act: "I have given you an example, that as I have done to you, so you do also." (*John* 13:15). Do not refer these words simply to what has taken place and to this example of humility, but also to all the actions of the life of Christ, for it is a very perfect mirror of all the virtues, and especially of that which is in this incident unfolded before us.

OF THE INSTITUTION OF THE MOST BLESSED SACRAMENT

To understand something of this mystery, remember to begin with that no human language can express the magnitude of the love which Christ has for His spouse, the Church, and which in consequence He has also for every soul in grace, seeing that each one such is also His spouse.

Thus it was that this very Tender Consort, when about to quit this life and leave His spouse, the Church, that His absence might not lead to forgetfulness, left as a memorial this Most Holy Sacrament in which He Himself resides, seeking no other thing than His own Self with which to perpetuate this mutual remembrance. During so long an absence He wished to leave His spouse a Companion, that she might never find herself alone, and thus He left to her this Sacrament in which He is Himself; and no better companion could He have found for her. He wished also to suffer death for His spouse and thus to redeem her and to enrich her with the price of His Blood. And that she might rejoice at will in this treasure, He has in this Sacrament left her the key, for as St. [John] Chrysostom tells us, "As often as we draw near to it, we should think we are laying our lips to the side of Christ and drinking His Precious Blood, and thus mingling our being with His." (Homil. 85, 3, *in Joan.*).

Moreover, this Heavenly Consort desired in return to be loved by His spouse with a very great love. To this end, He arranged this

Mystic Food, consecrated by such words that he who worthily receives it is both touched and wounded with this love.

He wished also to reassure His spouse, to give her pledges of this blest possession of glory, that compassed by this hope, she might traverse gaily the toiling bitterness of life; and in order that the spouse might hold as certain and assured this hope of blessedness, He left her this Ineffable Treasure as a pledge, equal in Itself to all she hopes for. Thus she need never despair of God's giving all to her in that state of glory and of spiritual existence, since He does not refuse it to her here in this valley of tears, where she lives in the flesh.

He willed also, at the hour of His death, to make a testament and leave to His spouse some resplendent gift, and so he left her the most precious thing He had and the most useful for her, since in this gift He left God to her. And finally, He wished to leave our souls a sufficient provision and nourishment on which to live, for the soul has no less need of special sustenance for her spiritual life than the body has for its physical life. Thus, it has come about that this Wise Physician, who knows so well the fluctuations of our feebleness, has instituted this Sacrament and set it in the form of nourishment. The very fashion of its institution shows us the effect which it accomplishes and the need which our souls have of It, similar indeed to the need our bodies have of suitable nourishment.[1]

Tuesday

THE PRAYER IN THE GARDEN, THE ARREST AND THE EVENTS BEFORE ANNAS

Today you will think of the prayer in the Garden, the seizing of the Saviour, and the entry into and the affronts endured in the house of Annas.

Consider in the first place how our Saviour, after the mysteries of the Supper were concluded, went with His disciples into the Garden of Olives to pray there before entering into the battle of His Passion. He did this in order to teach us how, in all the labors and temptations of this life, we should always have recourse to prayer, as to a sacred anchor. By His virtue, either the whole weight of tribulation will be lifted from us, or—and this is a yet greater grace—strength will be given us to support it.

On the way, He went in company with three disciples very dear to Him: St. Peter, St. James and St. John. These had been the

---

1. Cf. *The Exercises of St. Ignatius:* Third Week, First Contemplation.

witnesses of His glorious Transfiguration, and now they were themselves to see how different from the radiance of that vision would be the form He was about to assume for love of men. That they might see how the interior sufferings of His soul were no less than those which began to manifest themselves outwardly, He uttered these sad words: "My soul is sorrowful even unto death; stay you here and watch with Me." (*Matthew* 26:38). After these words, Our Lord withdrew Himself a stone's throw from His disciples, and prostrate on the ground, in an attitude of profound respect, He began His prayer, saying: "My Father, if it be possible, let this chalice pass from me. Nevertheless, not as I will, but as thou wilt." (*Matthew* 26:39). This prayer He recited three times, and at the third, He entered into such agony that He began to sweat drops of blood, which flowed all over His Sacred Body and threading their way down, dropped to the ground. Consider Our Lord in this sorrowful state, and see how the vision of Himself, in all the sufferings He is to endure, passes before His mind. He apprehends perfectly the very cruel torments which are being made ready for the most sensitive of human frames; He calls to mind all the sins of the world—[which are] the cause of His sufferings—and the ingratitude of so many souls who will fail to recognize this benefit and to profit by so great and costly a remedy. His soul is thus straitened in so many ways, His senses and most delicate frame so troubled that the muscles and members of His body become distended, and His sacred flesh opens on all sides and allows the blood to pass out in such abundance as to flow onto the ground. If the prospect of future suffering brings such anguish upon the body, what must be the state of the soul which directly comprehends it?

See now, when the prayer is finished, that a false friend arrives with his hateful company. He has forsworn his function of Apostle and become chief and captain of the army of Satan. Watch him as he steps out in front of all the others, and drawing near to the Good Master, barters Him away with a feigned kiss of peace. Then says Our Lord to those who have come to seize Him: "You are come out as it were to a robber, with swords and clubs to apprehend me. I sat daily with you teaching in the Temple, and you laid not hands upon me; but this is your hour, and the power of darkness." (*Matthew* 26:55; *Luke* 22:53). How amazing a mystery is this! What is more astonishing than to see the Son of God assume the figure, not merely of a sinner, but of a condemned criminal. "This," He says, "is your hour and the power of darkness," thus showing that the moment had come in which the most innocent Lamb was to be delivered into the power of the princes of darkness—that is, of the demons—to be subjected at the hands of their ministers to every torment and cruelty imaginable. Think to what depths of abasement this Divine Highness has lowered Himself for you, since He abandons Himself to the last of all evils, being delivered into the hands of devils. This is the pain your sins have deserved; He chooses to suffer it that you may be in a position to deliver yourself from it.

After these words, the whole troop of these hungry wolves lay hold upon this Gentle Lamb. Some seize Him on one side, some on another, each one as he may. Oh how roughly they treat Him; what insults they shower upon Him; how they push and strike Him; what cries and brawling, like that of hunters with their prey. They snatch those saintly hands which but a short time before had worked such miracles; they bind them strongly with running knots, but so awkwardly that the flesh of the arms is all torn and the blood flows. Thus, covered with ignominy, they drag Him through the public streets. Contemplate Him on this journey, separated from His disciples, surrounded by His enemies, hurried along at breakneck speed, breathing heavily, the features all strained, the face red and inflamed by the hurry of the march. And yet in the midst of this iniquitous treatment of His person, note the pervading calm of His figure, the gravity of His eyes, and that aspect wholly divine which, in the midst of the world's scorn, could yet never be obscured.

Come with Our Lord to the house of Annas: see how He answers courteously to the questions put to Him by the High Priest about His disciples and His doctrine, and how one of those wicked bystanders gave Him a great blow on the cheek, saying: "Answerest thou the High Priest so?" The Saviour replied gently: "If I have spoken evil, show me in what: if well, why strikest thou me?" (Cf. *John* 18:22-23). Admire here, O my Soul, not merely the mildness of this answer, but also that divine countenance, bruised and discolored by the force of the blow, the modesty of those serene eyes, that untroubled brow, and within, that Most Holy Soul, so humble and so ready, should the aggressor demand it, to turn the other cheek.[1]

---

1. See *The Exercises of St. Ignatius:* Third Week, Second Contemplation.

Wednesday

BEFORE CAIPHAS, THE DENIAL OF ST. PETER AND THE SCOURGING

Today you will think of Our Lord brought before the High Priest Caiphas, of the torments of that night, of the denial of St. Peter and of the Scourging at the Pillar.

Consider in the first place how Our Lord is led from the house of Annas, which He entered first, to that of the High Priest Caiphas. Bear Him company. See how the Sun of Justice is eclipsed and this divine face, on which the Angels desire to look, (Cf. *1 Peter* 1:12), is covered with spittle. The Saviour, adjured in the name of God to say who He was, replied as was fitting; but these men, unworthy of so noble an answer, are blinded by the splendor of so clear a light. They turn upon Him once more like wild beasts and pour forth their anger and their rage. They shower upon Him buffets and blows; with their vile mouths they spit upon this divine face; they cover His eyes with a blindfold, strike His Person and mock Him, saying, "Guess who struck thee." (Cf. *Luke* 22:64). Oh wonderful humility and patience of the Son of God! Oh this face, Beauty of the Angels, was it made to be spat upon? Men are accustomed to turn to some sordid corner when they wish to spit. In all this great palace was there no viler place to sully than Thy countenance? Can you, who are mere earth and dust, refrain, with this example before you, from humbling yourself?

Turn next to consider the sufferings the Saviour endured during this bitter night. The soldiers on guard mocked Him, as St. Luke tells us, and to master their inclination for sleep, they strike the Lord of Majesty and frolic with Him. See, O my Soul, how this most gentle Spouse serves as target for the arrows of all their blows and cuffs. Oh cruel night, weighted with woe! My Good Jesus, there was no sleep for You; neither did they slumber who found repose in tormenting You. Night was made that all creatures might find their rest in it and that sense and limb, wearied with the day's work, might be renewed. This is the moment those evil men chose to torment Your senses and Your limbs by wounding Your body, distressing Your soul, binding Your hands, buffeting Your face, spitting upon Your Person, offending Your ears, so that at the time when all the members are usually to be at rest, in You all suffer and are in pain. How different are these morning chants from those the Angels in Heaven are at this moment singing to You. There they sing, "Holy, Holy," and here, "Let him die, let him die." "Crucify him, crucify him." (*Luke* 23:21). O Angels in Paradise, you hear this double stream of sound. What feelings are yours as you watch Him being so maltreated on earth, toward whom you in Heaven are showing so much reverence? What must your thoughts be as you watch God bearing these sufferings for the sake of the very same persons who are inflicting them? Who has ever known an act of love like this—to suffer death in order to deliver from death the very ones who are causing it?

The torments of this sorrowful night grew greater still with the denial of St. Peter. This intimate friend, chosen to witness the glory of the Transfiguration, honored among all with the headship of the Church, he is the first of all, not once merely, but thrice, to swear and swear again, in the very presence of this same Lord, that he knew Him not, knew not even who He was. O Peter, and was He then so evil a Man there before you that you should feel so much ashamed of having known Him? You are to be the first to condemn Him, even before the High Priests, since you let it be understood that it is a dishonor to know Him. Could any deeper injury be done to Him than that? "And the Lord, turning, looked on Peter." (*Luke* 22:61). He cast His eyes upon this sheep that was lost. Oh glance of wonderful power—silent, but oh

how full of meaning. Well did Peter understand that language and the message of that
look. Vain had been the clamor of the cock to
arouse him, but not the clamor of those eyes;
and they do not merely speak, these eyes of
Christ, they work; the tears of Peter prove it,
tears which flow not so much from the eyes of
Peter as from the eyes of Christ.

And now, after these injuries, consider the
blows our Saviour received at the pillar. The
judge, seeing that he could not appease the
fury of that hellish crowd, decided to inflict
on Him so terrible a flagellation that it might
suffice to satisfy the rage of those cruel
hearts and that, contented with this, they
might no longer press for His death. Enter
now in spirit, O my Soul, into the praetorium
of Pilate; hold yourself ready to weep, for you
will indeed have need of tears at what you
are about to see and hear. See how inhu-
manly these vile and cruel executioners strip
our Saviour of His garments and how, with
great humility, He allows Himself to be thus
despoiled without opening His mouth or
answering a single word to all the insults
they shower upon Him. See how they fasten
His holy body to a pillar, that thus they may
be free to wound it just as they please, no
matter where or how. See the Lord of Angels
quite alone there, in the midst of these cruel

executioners, without friends of any kind or protectors to take His part, not even encountering from any eyes a glance of compassion. Watch how they begin at once with unmeasured cruelty to lay their rods and cords upon that most sensitive body; blow succeeds blow, bruise is added to bruise, gash to gash. Soon you will see this most holy body become a livid mass of wounds, the skin all torn away, the blood gushing forth and streaming down on all sides. But what must it be, above all, to see that great open wound between the shoulders, where the blows fall thickest?

The Scourging over, watch Our Lord clothing Himself again; from one corner of the hall to another He goes, picking up His garments in the presence of those cruel executioners, for none will serve or help Him; none will offer anything to soothe or refresh Him, as was usually done for those thus covered with wounds.

All these mysteries are well worthy of deep devotion, gratitude and thought.

Thursday

THE CROWNING WITH THORNS, THE *ECCE HOMO* AND THE CARRYING OF THE CROSS

Today we must think of the Crowning with Thorns, the *Ecce Homo,* and how the Saviour, pleading [sic], carries the Cross. In the *Book of Canticles* the Spouse thus invites us to the consideration of these sad mysteries: "Go forth, ye daughters of Sion, and see King Solomon in the diadem, wherewith his mother crowned him in the day of his espousals and in the day of the joy of his heart." (*Canticle of Canticles* 3:11).

O my Soul, what art thou doing? My Heart, what thoughts are thine? My Tongue, how art thou silent? O my most sweet Saviour, when I open my eyes and gaze upon this sorrowful scene as it unrolls itself before me, my heart is broken with grief. Are they not then sufficient, O Lord, those blows that are past, the death which is to come, and so much blood poured out already, that there should be need to drive in by force these thorns and draw from the head the blood the scourging has spared? To appreciate something of this so sorrowful a mystery, place first before thine eyes, O my Soul, the image of this Lord as He was before and the grandeur of His virtues, and then contrast these with the state in which He now is. See the splendor of His beauty, the gentleness of His eyes, the sweetness of His words, His air of authority, and with it all, His meekness, His calmness, and that peculiar aspect of His which commanded so much veneration.

After having studied and appreciated so finished a figure, turn thine eyes upon that which is now before thee, a figure clad in derisive purple, the reed as a royal sceptre in His hand, and upon His head this diadem of terror. His eyes are closed, His face as of one dead, and all His Person covered with blood and fouled throughout with what has been spat upon Him. View Him within and without, the heart seared with sorrow, the body torn with wounds, abandoned by His disciples, pursued by the Jews, an object of derision to the soldiers and of contempt to the High Priests, turned back by a wicked king, accused unjustly and deprived of all human good will. Do not think of all this as past and done with, but as something present; no sorrow, this, of another's, but your very own. Put yourself in the place of Him who suffers: think what you would suffer yourself if, in so sensitive a part as the head, many and sharp-pointed thorns were pressed in so deeply as to penetrate to the bone. Thorns indeed! Why, the simple prick of a pin is scarely endurable. What then must this head have suffered, itself so sensitive, and yet subjected to such a string of torments?

The Crowning with Thorns over and the Mocking of the Saviour finished, the judge takes Him by the hand, and all battered as

He is, brings Him face-to-face with the furious crowd, saying, *Ecce Homo*—"Behold the Man." It was as much as to say: If it were through envy you sought His death, see Him now, an object of envy no longer, but of pity. You feared He might make Himself king; see Him now so disfigured He hardly carries the semblance of a man. From these torn hands what do you dread? From this racked frame what more do you demand?

From this thou mayest form an idea, O my Soul, of what the Saviour looked like, since the judge thought it enough to expose that figure to soften thereby even such enemies as His. Thou mayest well understand how evil a thing it is to have no Christian compassion for the sufferings of Christ, since they were such as might—so the judge thought—have brought a feeling of tenderness even into those proud hearts.

Pilate, seeing how all that had been already inflicted on that Most Holy Lamb had not yet sufficed to calm the fury of His enemies, entered into the praetorium and seated himself on his judgment seat to pronounce the final sentence. Even now the Cross was ready at the gates, and this terrible banner appeared aloft, menacing the Saviour's head. The cruel sentence is pronounced and promulgated. His enemies add cruelty to cruelty, for they lay upon these shoulders, bruised and torn by blows, the plank of the Cross. The gentle Saviour refuses not this burden, laden with all our sins; rather, with unbounded charity and obedience, He embraces it for love of us.

The "Innocent Isaac" advances toward the place of sacrifice, bearing this heavy burden upon His failing shoulders. A large crowd follows Him, and many holy women accompany Him, weeping. Who indeed would not shed tears at seeing the King of Angels moving forward step-by-step, with this weighty load upon Him, His knees trembling, His body bent, the eyes almost closed, the face all smeared with blood, and this "garland" about His head, in the midst of a shameless clamor and of outcries against Him.

And now, my Soul, turn thine eyes away awhile from this cruel spectacle. Hasten with all speed and sobbing breath and weeping eyes and seek the house of the Virgin. When thou hast found her, cast thyself at her feet, and begin to say to her in accents of grief: "Our Lady of the Angels, Queen of Heaven, Gate of Paradise, Advocate of the World, Refuge of Sinners, Salvation of the Just, Joy of the Saints, Mistress of all Virtues, Mirror of Purity, Ensign of Chastity, Model of Patience and Sum of all Perfections, woe is me, my Lady, that my sight should have been preserved to see this hour. How shall I live longer, now that my eyes have witnessed that which has just passed before them? What further need of words. I come from thine only Son and my Lord, and He was in the midst of friends of mine, carrying the Cross on which He is to be crucified."

Who can fathom now the Virgin's grief? Her soul faints away; her face and all her virginal body is bathed in a deadly sweat, which would indeed have borne her life away had not the will of God preserved her for a yet greater martyrdom and a more glorious crown. Forth she goes, this Virgin, in search of her Son. The longing to see Him gives back to her the strength of which grief had deprived her. She hears from afar the clash of arms, the tramp of many feet and the voices of the city criers making proclamation. Soon she catches sight on high of the lance-heads and halberds and perceives on the ground drops and traces of blood, which suffice without other guide to show where her Son has passed. Nearer and nearer does she draw to this beloved Son of hers; she lifts up her eyes, darkened with sorrow and the shadow of death, to catch a glimpse, if she can, of One who so loved her soul. Oh, what dread and longing are mingled in Mary's heart—at one moment longing to see Him, at the next shrinking back with dread, lest she might see a sight so lamentable.

At length she arrives at a spot where she can see Him; one upon the other gaze, these two lights of Heaven; to the inmost heart do their looks penetrate, revealing that which stirs to the depths their compassionate souls. Silent are their lips, but the Mother's heart spoke, and her very gentle Son made answer: "Why hast thou come here, my Beloved, my very dearest and my Mother? Thy sorrow increases mine; thy torments torture me. Return, My Mother, return to thy house. Thy modesty and virginal purity are ill-suited to the company of murderers and thieves." Such, and others more touching still, were the words which these hearts, so full of compassion, addressed one to the other; and thus was the toilsome journey completed to the place of crucifixion.

Friday

THE CRUCIFIXION AND THE SEVEN WORDS

Today we must contemplate the mystery of the Cross and the Seven Words of Our Lord therefrom. Arouse thyself now, O my Soul, and set thyself to consider the mystery of the Holy Cross, of which the fruit has made good the evil caused by the poisoned fruit of the forbidden tree.

Firstly, see our Saviour arrived now at the place of execution. His depraved enemies, desirous of making His death more shameful still, strip Him of all His garments, including the inner tunic, which was all woven in one piece without seam. Mark with what meekness this most innocent Lamb allows Himself to be despoiled, without opening His mouth or breathing one single word against those who were thus maltreating Him. Rather is it with a very good will that He consents to be stripped of His garments, to bear the shame of nakedness, for it is thus that He may reclothe, better far than with the leaves of a fig tree, the nakedness into which we fell by sin.

Certain learned writers tell us that, to remove Our Lord's tunic, they took off with great cruelty the Crown of Thorns upon His head; and once He was stripped, replaced it again, driving in the thorns deeply for the second time, and thus causing Him the greatest suffering. It is quite conceivable that this cruelty was practiced upon Christ together with all those other ones, and some so unusual which they made Him undergo during the course of His Passion—especially as the Evangelist tells us that they did to Him all they would. Then, the tunic was already clinging close to the wounds caused by the Scourging, and the blood had congealed and become attached to the garment, so that when they stripped Him—so completely were these evil men devoid of pity—they tore it off with one wrench and with such force that they opened again and renewed all those wounds of the Scourging in such a manner that this holy body lay open, as it were, flayed on all sides, leaving nothing but one vast wound, pouring out blood from every part.

Consider here, O my Soul, the grandeur of the divine bounty and mercy which both shine forth in this mystery with such resplendence. He who spreads the sky with clouds and the fields with flowers and beauty is Himself despoiled of His garments. Think of the cold this Holy Body must have suffered, all shattered as it was and stript, not merely of clothes, but of skin, and open on every side with gaping wounds. St. Peter, the previous night, clad as he was and standing by a fire, yet felt the cold. How much more must this most sensitive body have suffered, all nakedness and wounds?

Consider how our Saviour was nailed to the Cross. Think of the anguish He must have endured as these thick, bent nails pass through the most sensitive and delicate parts of a most sensitive frame. Think of the Virgin

Mary, who sees with her eyes and hears with her ears the blows, hard and cruel, as they fall one by one upon these divine limbs. Truly, these blows of the hammer and these nails that pierce the hands of the Son are wounding yet more the heart of the Mother.

See now how they raise the Cross on high and make ready to drop it into the hole which has been prepared for it, and how these cruel executioners, at the given moment, let it fall with a jerk, causing the whole Sacred Body to shake violently in the air and thus enlarging the wounds of the nails with intolerable pain.

O my Saviour and Redeemer, what heart, though it be of stone, will not but share this torment? For indeed, on that day the very rocks were rent asunder on beholding Your sufferings on the Cross. The sorrows of death have surrounded You, O Lord, and all the winds and waves of the sea have encompassed You. (Cf. *Psalms* 17:5). You have been engulfed in the depths of the abyss, and there is no sure standing for You. (Cf. *Psalms* 68:3). Your Father has forsaken You; (*Matthew* 27:46); what look You for, O Lord, from men? Your enemies cry out against You; Your friends break Your heart; Your soul is troubled; and for love of me, You admit no consolation. Stubborn indeed were my sins; Your expiation is evidence of this. I behold You, O my King, fastened to this beam, with nothing to sustain You but these three nails of iron; they alone support Your Sacred Body; there is no rest for You but on them. When You allow the weight of the body to rest upon the feet, You only widen more the wounds of the feet with the nails that pierce them. Would You use the hands as a support? Then the whole weight on the body serves but to enlarge also these wounds in the hands. Your Sacred Head, tormented and weakened by the Crown of Thorns, what cushion is there to support it! O how willingly, Virgin most serene, would thine arms have fulfilled this office, but no arms of thine can serve here, only the arms of the Cross. Upon them will this Sacred Head recline when it would be at rest, and the only solace it will have will be to dig in deeper yet the thorns into the skull.

The presence of the Mother increased still more the sorrows of the Son. Thereby was His heart rent within, no less than was His Sacred Body without. O good Jesus, there are indeed two crosses for You this day, one for the body and one for the soul; one, the outward passion; the other, compassion; the one pierces the body with iron nails; the other, Thy most holy soul with nails of sorrow. Who can declare, O good Jesus, what You felt as

You recognized the anguish of that most holy soul which clung so closely with You to the Cross, when You saw this devoted soul pierced through and through with a sword of sorrow, when You turned toward her those bleeding eyes and gazed on that sacred face enveloped in the bitterness of death and watched the anguish of that soul so near to death, nay, to worse than death, and the streaming tears that flowed from those eyes most pure, and when you heard the groans drawn from that sacred heart under so desperate a weight of grief.

Now you may consider the Seven Words pronounced by Our Lord from the Cross. Of these, the first was: "Father, forgive them, for they know not what they do." (*Luke* 23:34). The second was addressed to the thief: "This day thou shalt be with me in paradise." (*Luke* 23:43). And the third to His most holy Mother: "Woman, behold thy Son." (*John* 19:26). The fourth: "I thirst." (*John* 19:28). The fifth: "My God, my God, why hast thou forsaken me?" (*Matthew* 27:46). The sixth: "It is consummated." (*John* 19:30). The seventh: "Father, into thy hands I commend my spirit." (*Luke* 23:46).

Consider, O my Soul, with what charity He commends His enemies to the Father with these words; with what mercy He welcomes the thief who recognized Him; with what immense love He recommends His pious Mother to the Beloved Disciple; with what thirsting zeal He witnesses to His longing for the salvation of men; in what sorrowful tones He pronounces His prayer and lays His griefs before the Divine Majesty; how to the end He remains in the most perfect submission to the Father; and finally how He recommends His soul to Him and resigns Himself completely into His most holy keeping.

It is clear how in each one of these words is found a lesson of virtue. The first recommends to us charity toward our enemies. The second, mercy toward sinners. The third, dutifulness toward our parents. The fourth, the desire of our neighbor's salvation. The fifth, prayer in the midst of tribulations and abandonment by God. The sixth, the virtue of obedience and perseverance. The seventh, perfect resignation [of ourselves] into the hands of God, in whom lies our whole perfection.

Saturday

THE PIERCING WITH THE LANCE, THE
TAKING DOWN FROM THE CROSS, THE
SORROWS OF MARY AND THE BURIAL

Today think of the Saviour pierced with a lance, of the taking down from the Cross, of the tears of Our Lady, and of the laying in the the tomb.

Consider how our Saviour has now expired upon the Cross and accomplished the desires of His cruel enemies, who wished to see Him die. But for all that, the flame of their wrath is not extinguished. Still do they seek to wreak vengeance upon Him. They set furiously upon these holy relics, dividing among themselves and casting lots for His garments, and piercing His sacred side with the cruel blow of a lance. O savage servants! O hearts of iron! Did the sufferings of the living body seem so slight to you, that you would not even let Him be in death? What rage or enmity [was] so great that it is not sated at sight of the enemy dead before its face? Lift up for a moment your cruel eyes and see this lifeless figure, these sightless eyes, this pallid countenance, this shadowed bitterness of death: are you then harder than iron or the diamond, that this sight does not soften you?

And now the soldier advances, lance in hand and, with all his strength, plunges it into the bare breast of the Saviour. The Cross shakes in the air with the force of the blow, and there gush forth water and blood for the healing of the world's sin. O river flowing out from Paradise and inundating all the earth with thy streams! O Wound in the Sacred Side, caused by love for men rather than by the iron of the lance! O Gateway of Heaven, and Avenue of Paradise, Refuge and Fortified Tower, Sanctuary of the Just, Last Resting Place of the Pilgrim, Nest for the Spotless Doves and Flowered Bed of the Spouse of Solomon! Hail, O Wound in that Precious Side which rends devout hearts, Wound which pierces the souls of the just, Rose of Beauty unspeakable, Ruby of Priceless Worth, Door into the Heart of Christ, Witness of His love and Pledge of Eternal Life!

Consider now, how at the close of this same day, those two holy persons arrived, Joseph and Nicodemus. They set their ladders to the Cross and lifted down in their arms the body of the Saviour. When the Virgin saw that an end had come to the torments of the Passion and that this Sacred Body was being lowered to the ground, she prepared herself to assure it a safe refuge in her arms and from the arms of the Cross to receive it into her own. So with great humility she asked these noble personages that, as she had not been able to bid her Son adieu nor to receive His last embrace as He died upon the Cross, she might now be allowed to approach. She begged them not to add to her desolation and, though His enemies would not leave Him to her living, that His friends would not deny

Him to her in death. The Virgin then takes Him in her arms, and what words can voice all she felt? O Angels of peace, weep with this holy Virgin; weep, ye skies; ye stars of Heaven, weep; and all ye creatures of earth, join with Mary in her lamentations. The Mother embraces that shattered body, gathers it closely to her breast—she has no strength but for that—and lays her head amid the thorns of that sacred brow. Body to body, the figure of this most holy Mother is stained with the Son's blood, and that of the Son steeped in the Mother's tears. O gentle Mother, is this then truly your Most Sweet Child? Is this He whom you conceived in such glory and bore with such joy? Where are the joys of the past? Your delights of bygone days, where are they? Is this that Mirror of Beauty on which you gazed?

All round about were weeping; the holy women were in tears, and those noble men; Heaven and earth were weeping, and all creatures shared the Virgin's tears. The holy Evangelist wept too and embraced the body of his Master, saying: "O good Master, O my Lord, who now henceforth will guide me? Before whom shall I lay my doubts? On whose breast shall I recline? Who will share with me the secrets of Heaven? What staggering change is this? Last night you pressed me to your Sacred Heart and gave the joy of life to me; and now I repay so great a gift by holding you lifeless in my arms. Is that the face I gazed on, transfigured on Mount Thabor? Is this the figure which then was brighter than the sun at noon?"

That holy woman, a sinner once, wept also and, embracing the Saviour's feet, exclaimed: "O Light of my eyes and Healing of my soul, wearied with sin, as you see me, who will now receive me, who will heal my wounds, who will answer for me, who will defend me from the Pharisees? O how different were these feet when I washed them and you welcomed me as I knelt! O Beloved of my heart, who will tell me that I may die with You? O Life of my soul, how can I say I love You since—though holding You dead before my eyes—I yet live?"

Thus, all that holy company wept and lamented, bathing and cleansing with their tears this Sacred Body. As the moment of burial approached, they enveloped the Holy Body in a white winding-sheet, covered the head with a linen cloth, and then, placing it on a stretcher, made their way toward the tomb. There they laid this Precious Treasure; the sepulchre was closed with a stone, and the Mother's heart with a dark cloud of sorrow. There for the second time she separates herself from her Son and once again feels her loneliness; there she sees herself despoiled of all her Good; there, where her treasure is, her heart lies buried.

Sunday

THE DESCENT INTO LIMBO, THE APPEARANCES OF OUR LORD AND THE ASCENSION

Today you may think of the descent of Our Lord into Limbo, of the appearance to Our Lady, to the holy Magdalen and to the disciples; and finally of the mystery of the glorious Ascension.

As for the first point [the descent into Limbo], consider how great is the joy of the holy patriarchs in Limbo on this day at the coming and presence among them of their Liberator, and what thanks and praise they offer Him for a salvation so long desired and hoped for. Those who come back to Spain from the East Indies tell us that they look on the time spent during the voyage as well employed on account of the delight they feel when they reach land. If this is true of such a journey as that and after an exile of one or two years, what must it be after an exile of three or four thousand years when the day comes on which so great a salvation is secured and on which is reached the harbor of the land of the living?

Consider also the joy which the most holy

Virgin experienced when on this day she received the visit of her risen Son. Certainly, as it was she who felt most deeply the sorrows of His Passion, so it is she who will taste most fully the joy of His Resurrection. What must her feelings have been as before her she beheld her Son, living and glorious, attended by all those holy patriarchs risen with Him? What does she do? What does she say? How she embraces Him and kisses Him, tears falling all the while from those devoted eyes. Oh, the longing to go with Him, if this grace might be granted to her!

Think of the joy of the holy Marys, and especially of her who lingered weeping at the tomb, waiting for the Beloved of her soul, that she might cast herself at His feet and speak with Him, living and risen, whom in death she had longed for and sought. Note well that, after His Mother, it is to her He first appears, for she loved Him more than the rest, and sought Him with more persevering care and more abundant tears; and so you may hold it as certain that you too will speak with God if you seek Him with tears and care like hers.

Consider how He appeared in the guise of a pilgrim to the disciples who were going to Emmaus; with what affability He joins them, with what familiarity He accompanies them, how gently He conceals His identity from them, and then with what love He reveals Himself to them and leaves them with a sweetness as of honey upon their lips. Let your conversation resemble theirs; speak with compassionate sorrow, as did they, of the anguish and pain of Christ, and you may be sure His accompanying presence will never fail you, if you bear within you always the memory of Him.

As concerning the mystery of the Ascension, consider how Our Lord delayed His entry into Heaven for forty days, during which time He frequently appeared to His disciples and taught them and spoke with them of the kingdom of God. He did not then ascend to Heaven and separate Himself from them before they were ready themselves to ascend in spirit with Him. This shows us that often the actual presence of Christ—*i.e.,* the consoling *feeling* of devotion—is withdrawn from those who, rising high in spiritual flight, are thereby secured the more against danger. Herein is wonderfully evident the Providence of God and the manner He has of dealing differently with His own at various times. He coaxes the weak with favors; the strong He puts to the test. For the tiny ones there is milk; the bigger ones are weaned. Some He consoles, the others He proves, treating each one according to the measure of his progress. Consequently, he who is regaled with devotion should not presume, for [this] favor is a sign of his [own] weakness; and one in desolation should not lose courage, since it is often a sign of [his] strength.

In the presence of His disciples and while they were *looking on,* He ascends to Heaven, that thus they may be witnesses of these mysteries; and there is no better witness to the works of God than he who knows of them by experience. If you would truly know how good God is, how gracious and gentle with His own, and of what kind is the virtue and efficacy of His grace, of His love, of His providence and of His consolations, ask it of those who have had experience thereof, and they will give you a very convincing testimony.[1]

The Saviour also wished His disciples to see Him mounting to Heaven, that they might follow Him with their eyes and in spirit, that they might realize [from] the parting and experience some loneliness from His absence, such being the best preparation for the reception of His grace. Eliseus demanded of Elias his spirit, and this good master replied: "If thou see me when I am taken from

_____
1. As was precisely the case with St. Teresa when she sought St. Peter's counsel and advice. See Ch. xxx of her *Life,* written by herself.

thee, thou shalt have what thou hast asked."
(*4 Kings* 2:10). The heirs of the spirit of
Christ will be those whose love will make
them feel the departure of Christ, who will
suffer from His absence, and who, throughout
this exile, will be forever sighing after His
presence. Such [are] the feelings of that holy
man who says: "You have been my consoler,
but no adieu have you bade me; all along the
way you have blessed your own, and nothing
for me; Angels have promised that you will
come back again, but nothing do I hear."

What was the loneliness, the grief, the
lamentations and tears of the most holy Virgin, of the Beloved Disciple, of St. [Mary]
Magdalen, and of all the Apostles as they
watched fade away from their sight the One
who had stolen their hearts? Yet we are told
that they went back to Jerusalem with great
joy, for they loved Him much; and indeed, it
was this same love which, though it made
them feel the parting, led them on the other
hand to rejoice in His glory; for true love
seeks not itself, but rather the object of its
love.

It remains to consider with what glory and
joy and hymns of praise this Noble Victor was
received into His heavenly city and how fes-
tive was the reception He met with. Men and
Angels unite together and move forward

toward this noble city, once again to repeople a spot deserted for so many years. Christ, in His most sacred humanity, advances above them all and goes to seat Himself at the right hand of the Father. How much there is to ponder here. We see how well employed are those who labor for the love of God, and how He who humbles Himself and suffers more than any other is glorified and raised higher than all. Thus, those enamored of true glory know well the road they must take to arrive there—which is to go down, that they may ascend and to submit themselves to all, that they may be elevated above all.[1]

CHAPTER 5

Six Parts Which May Enter into the Exercise of Prayer

Such then, Christian Reader, are the meditations in which you may exercise yourself during each day of the week, and thus there should be no lack of matter for reflection. It should be borne in mind, however, that the meditation may be preceded and followed by certain other kindred and appropriate

---

1. See *The Exercises of St. Ignatius:* Fourth Week, First Contemplation.

exercises.

In the first place, before beginning the meditation, it is necessary to prepare the heart for this holy exercise, as one might tune up a guitar before playing on it.

After the preparation comes the reading over of the subject of the meditation for that day, according to the order we have indicated for the days of the week. This is certainly necessary for beginners and until one is familiar with subjects of meditation.

The meditation may be followed by a devout act of thanksgiving for benefits received and by an offering of our whole life and of that of Christ our Saviour in return for them.

Finally comes the petition—prayer, strictly so called—in which we ask for what we need and for our salvation, together with that of our neighbor and of the whole Church.

These six acts[1] may well find a place in prayer. Among other advantages they serve to furnish a man with abundant matter for carrying the exercise forward and to offer

---

1. Viz., preparation, reading, meditation, thanksgiving, offering and petition. Clearly we have here the familiar and simplest of all *schemes* of mental prayer, which groups the exercise into three sections: 1) the preparation, 2) the *discursive* part, *i.e.,* reading or thinking about the subject matter, 3) the *affections,* of which St. Peter enumerates three.

him various kinds of nourishment, so that if he cannot partake of one, he may partake of another, and if he lose the thread of the meditation at any point, another is at hand on which to continue.

I know quite well that all these acts, and in the order given, are not always necessary, but still they serve as a start for beginners by giving them a definite order to follow and a scheme by which they may direct themselves. Again, in all I have said so far, I would not be considered as laying down a permanent rule or general law, for my intention is not to legislate, but to introduce newcomers into this path. Once they have entered upon it, use and experience—and most of all the Holy Spirit—will teach them the rest.

CHAPTER 6

The Preparation Required Before Prayer

At this point it will be useful to treat individually of each one of the above-mentioned acts and, to begin with, [to treat] of the preparation, which comes first of all.

Coming to the place where you are to pray, take up a position on your knees or standing, or with arms extended in the form of a cross, or prostrate on the ground, or seated, should you be unable to manage otherwise. Then begin with the Sign of the Cross, and get your imagination under control, withdrawing it from the affairs of daily life, raising up your soul on high and considering how Our Lord is watching you. Maintain in yourself the same attention and respect as if you saw Him actually present. Make a general *Act of Contrition,* if it is the morning meditation, and say the *Confiteor.* If it is in the evening, examine your conscience on all your thoughts, words, actions and omissions, and on your forgetfulness of Our Lord, grieving over the defects of that day and of all your life, humbling yourself before the Majesty of God, in whose presence you stand; and you will say these words of the holy Patriarch: "I will speak to my Lord, whereas I am but dust and ashes." (*Genesis* 18:27). Then you will say these verses of the Psalms: (*Psalms* 122:1-3).

To thee have I lifted up my eyes, who dwellest in Heaven.
Behold, as the eyes of servants are on the hands of their masters,
As the eyes of the handmaid are on the hands of her mistress,
So are our eyes unto the Lord our God
Until he have mercy on us.

Have mercy on us, O Lord, have mercy on us.
Glory be to the Father . . .

Moreover, as we are not able of ourselves to frame one single good thought, "but our sufficiency is from God," (*2 Corinthians* 3:5), and as none can invoke worthily the name of Jesus without the help of the Holy Spirit, let us say:

Come, most sweet Spirit, and send forth from Heaven a ray of Thy light. Come, Father of the poor; come, Giver of gifts; come, Illuminator of hearts; Come, Best of Consolers, Gentle Guest of the soul and Rest thereof. Thou art our Repose in toil, our Refreshment in the heat of the day, our Consolation in the midst of tears. O most blessed Light, fill the hearts of the Faithful.

V. Send forth Thy spirit and they shall be created.
R. And Thou shalt renew the face of the earth.

O God, Who hast instructed the hearts of the Faithful by the light of the Holy Spirit, grant us in the same Spirit to be always truly wise and ever to rejoice in His consolation, through Christ our Lord. Amen.

These prayers said, beg Our Lord to give you the grace to remain there with that attention and devotion, with that interior recollection, with that fear and reverence which befit this Sovereign Majesty, and that you may spend this time of prayer in such manner as to come forth therefrom with renewed strength and ready for everything in His service. Prayer which does not at once produce this fruit is very imperfect and almost valueless.[1]

CHAPTER 7

The Reading

When the preparation is finished, the next thing is the reading over of the meditation which is to form the subject-matter of our prayer. This must not be done hurriedly nor in cursory fashion, but with attention and calm, applying thereto not merely one's intelligence, in order to understand what is read, but above all, the will, in order to relish it. And when one alights on some moving passage, one should pause a little to appreciate it better. The reading should not be very long. Thus, a longer time will be available for the meditation, which is all the more profitable in proportion as one ponders more leisurely on what is read and enters more devoutly into its spirit.

---

1. See *The Exercises of St. Ignatius: Additions,* First Week, iii and iv.

However, should the heart be too distracted for prayer, one may delay a little longer over the reading, or combine reading with meditation, reading a passage and then meditating on it, reading another and meditating on that, and so on. The mind, fixed on the words of the book, does not so easily wander away on all sides as when free and untrammeled; but better still is it to combat and scorn these distracting thoughts and to go on struggling in the work of prayer (like Jacob of old, who strove throughout the night). (Cf. *Genesis* 32:24). The contest will cease in the end and victory will be won, and Our Lord will give us devotion, or some even greater grace, for He never refuses Himself to such as combat faithfully.

CHAPTER 8

The Meditation

After the reading comes the meditation on what we have just read. There are some subjects which may be visualized by the imagination, such as all the scenes in the Life and Passion of Christ, the Last Judgment, Hell and Heaven. Others pertain rather to the understanding than to the imagination—for example, the benefits of God, His goodness and mercy, or any other of His perfections which we may choose to consider. This kind of meditation is called *intellectual,* and the other *imaginative.* We are accustomed in these exercises to use the one or the other, according as the subject-matter demands.

When the meditation is *imaginative,* we must figure each detail as it actually exists, or actually happens, and must consider it as taking place in the very spot where we are and in our presence. Such a representation will make our consideration and appreciation of the mystery more vivid. It will be even better to imagine all as taking place within our own hearts. If cities and kingdoms can find a place there, how much more a representation of these mysteries. This will help a great deal in keeping the soul recollected by occupying it within itself (like the bee in her hive, busy over her honey); for to go in thought to Jerusalem and to meditate upon these mysteries there, where they took place, is something which usually causes headache and weariness. Consequently, no one should fix the imagination too intently on what he is considering, lest so forceful an application should strain his natural powers.

CHAPTER 9

The Thanksgiving

After the meditation comes the act of thanksgiving. We should take the occasion of the meditation just concluded to thank Our Lord for the benefit conferred on us in the mystery we have been considering. Thus, if the meditation has been on the Passion, we ought to thank Our Lord for having, with so much toil, redeemed us; if it has been on sin, for having waited so long for our repentance; if on the miseries of this life, for having spared us so many; if on the moment of death, for delivering us from the dangers thereof and for having waited for us to repent; if on the glory of Heaven, for having made it so perfect; and so on for the rest.

To these benefits should be joined all those others of which we have spoken already: creation, preservation, redemption, vocation, etc. Thus, each one should thank Our Lord for having made him in His image and likeness; for giving him memory, wherewith he may call God to mind; and the understanding, with which to know Him; and the will, with which to love Him; for giving him an Angel, to guard him from so many pains and perils, from many mortal sins and from dying in sin (which is nothing less than a delivery from eternal death); for having deigned Himself to assume our nature and to die for us; for having caused him to be born of Christian parents; for the gift of holy Baptism; for the gift of grace here and the promise of glory [hereafter]; and for having received him as His adopted son; for having fitted him out in the Sacrament of Confirmation with arms with which to combat the world, the flesh and the devil; for having given us Himself in the Sacrament of the Altar; and for having placed within reach the Sacrament of Penance, whereby grace lost through mortal sin may be recovered; and finally, for the many good inspirations He has given in the past, and still gives; and for the assistance accorded us to pray and work well and to persevere in the good begun. To these benefits join those others, general and particular, which you recognize as having been received from Our Lord. For these and all others, open as well as hidden, render as much thanks as possible and summon all created things in Heaven and on earth to help you in this work. To this end you may recite, if you wish, this canticle:

> All ye works of the Lord, bless the Lord;
> Praise and exalt him above all forever.
> —*Daniel* 3:57

Or this Psalm:

Bless the Lord, O my soul, and let all that is within me bless his holy name.

Bless the Lord, O my soul, and never forget all he hath done for thee.

Who forgiveth all thy iniquities; who healeth all thy diseases.

Who redeemeth thy life from destruction; who crowneth thee with mercy and compassion.

—*Psalms* 102:1-4

CHAPTER 10

The Offering

When we have given heartfelt thanks to Our Lord for all these benefits, there naturally rises within us that feeling which the prophet David expressed in the words, "What shall I render to the Lord for all the things that he hath rendered to me?" (*Psalms* 115:12). A man may in some measure satisfy this desire by giving on his part and offering to God everything that he has and is able to offer.

To this end, he should, in the first place, offer himself as His servant forever, resigning and placing himself in His hands, so that He may do with him whatsoever He would, in time and in eternity. Let him offer, at the same time, all his words, actions, thoughts and toils, all he may have to bear and suffer, that all may be to the honor and glory of God's holy Name.

Secondly, offer to the Father all the merits and good works of His Son; all the toils He, in obedience, underwent in this world, from the Crib to the Cross, for it is all our treasure and heritage which He has bequeathed to us in the New Testament, by which He has made us heirs to all this great wealth. For just as what is given me by grace is no less mine than what I win myself by my own efforts, so the merits and rights which He has given me belong to me as much as if I had myself sweated and labored to secure them. Thus may a man make this second offering no less than the former, counting up as his own all the services and labors and all the virtues of that most holy life, His obedience, His patience, His humility, His loyalty, His love, His mercy and all the rest. This is the richest and most precious offering we can possibly make to God.[1]

---

1. See in *The Exercises of St. Ignatius* the well-known prayer *Sume et suscipe,* in the *Contemplation for Obtaining Love:* Fourth Week.

CHAPTER 11

The Petition

After making so rich an offering, we may confidently anticipate a prompt recompense. And firstly, with a deep sentiment of charity and with zeal for the honor of Our Lord, let us beg that all peoples and nations of the world may know Him, praise and adore Him as their own true God and Lord, saying with all our hearts these words of the prophet: "Let people confess to thee, O God; let all people give praise to thee." (*Psalms* 66:4).

Pray also for the heads of the Church— viz., the Pope, Cardinals and Bishops—and for all the other ministers and lower prelates, that Our Lord may direct and enlighten them in such a manner that they may lead all men to know and obey their Creator. Also, as St. Paul counsels us, we should pray for kings, and all holding similar positions of dignity, that through their fore-sight we may pass quiet and tranquil lives. This is well pleasing to God, Our Lord, "Who will have all men to be saved and to come to the knowledge of the truth." (*1 Timothy* 2:4).

Let us pray also for all the members of His Mystical Body: for the good, that Our Lord may preserve them; for sinners, that He may convert them; for the dead, that He may mercifully free them from all toil and lead them to the repose of eternal life. Let us ask also for all poor people and the infirm, for those in prison and captives, that through the merits of His Son God may help them and deliver them from evil.

Having prayed for our neighbor, let us also pray for ourselves. Each one's individual necessity will make clear what ought to be asked for, if one knows himself well. However, that there may be no obscurity in this matter, the following are the graces for which we may beg.

Firstly, through the merits and sufferings of Our Lord, let us beg pardon for all our sins and contrition for them, and especially let us ask for help against all those passions and vices toward which we incline the most and are most tempted, disclosing all our wounds to the Heavenly Physician, that He may heal and cure them with the unction of His grace.

Then, secondly, let us ask for those very lofty and noble virtues in which is contained the sum of all Christian perfection—viz., faith, hope, love, fear, humility, patience, obedience, courage to face every toil, poverty of spirit, contempt of the world, discretion, purity of intention and other similar virtues which lie at the summit of this spiritual edifice. Faith is the primary root of all Christian life; hope is the prop and remedy in all the temptations of life; love is the culminating point of all Christian perfection; the fear of God is the beginning of true wisdom; humility is the foundation of all virtues; patience is a shield against the blows and assaults of the enemy; obedience is a most agreeable offering, by which a man offers himself in sacrifice to God; discretion is the eye of the soul to enlighten and direct her in every path; courage is her arm for the accomplishment of every labor; and purity of intention refers and directs all our actions toward God.

Thirdly, let us also pray for those other virtues which, without being of themselves the most important, help nevertheless to preserve the latter—viz., temperance in eating and drinking, restraint of the tongue, custody of the senses, a modest and composed deportment, courtesy of manner and good example toward one's neighbor, rigor and austerity toward oneself, and other similar good qualities.

After this, conclude with the prayer for the love of God; dwell upon this; occupy with this the greater part of your time; demand of Our Lord this virtue with feelings of the most ardent longing, for herein lies all our good. Thus may you pray:

SPECIAL PRAYER FOR THE LOVE OF GOD

Above all these virtues, grant me, O Lord, Thy grace, that I may love Thee with my whole heart, with my whole soul, with all my strength and with my whole being, for thus Thou dost bid me do. Oh, Thou art all my Hope and all my Glory, my one Refuge, my whole Joy! O Best Beloved of all, Spouse emblossomed, honeyed and sweet: O Sweetness of my heart, Life of my soul, joyous Resting Place of my spirit! O Day of Eternity, beautiful and bright, my Innermost Light serene, Flowering Paradise of my heart, my Creator, most lovable and all sufficient for me!

Make ready, O my God, make ready, O Lord, a pleasing dwelling place within me for Thyself, that according to the promise of Thy Holy Word, Thou mayest come to me and rest with me. Mortify in me all that is displeasing to Thy sight, and make of me a man according to Thy own heart. Wound, O Lord, my inmost soul with the arrows of Thy love, and inebriate it with the wine of Thy perfect charity. Ah! When will that be? When shall I please Thee in all things? When shall I be dead to all in me that displeases Thee? When shall I be wholly Thine? When shall I cease to be my own? When shall nothing but Thyself live in me? When shall I love Thee most ardently? When will the flame of Thy love enkindle me wholly? When shall I be wholly softened and carried away by Thy most potent sweetness? When wilt Thou open Thyself to this poor mendicant and discover to him Thy most lovely kingdom, which is within me, which is Thyself, with all Thy treasures? When wilt Thou ravish me and sweep me off, transport me and hide me in Thyself, so that anything of myself appears no more? When—free of these impeding chains—wilt thou make me a spirit with Thee, that nothing may thus separate me from Thee anymore?

O Beloved, Beloved, Beloved of my soul! O Sweetness, Sweetness of my heart! Hearken to me, O Lord, not for any merits of mine, but of Thine infinite bounty. Teach me, enlighten me, guide and help me in all things, so that nothing may be done or said but what is pleasing in Thy sight. O my God, my Loved One and the Innermost Good of my soul! O Love so sweet to me! O Delight so great for me! O my Strength, help me; my Light, guide me!

O God of my heart! Why dost Thou not

bestow Thyself on one so poor? Thou fillest earth and sky, and yet my heart is empty. Thou dost clothe the lilies of the field; Thou dost feed the little birds; Thou dost support the worms; why dost Thou forget me, I who have forgotten all things for Thee? Late have I known thee, O Infinite Goodness! Late have I loved Thee, O Beauty so ancient and so new! How sad the time when I loved Thee not! How sad, myself, when I knew Thee not; how blind when I did not see Thee! Thou art within me, and I sought Thee without! But since at long last I have found Thee, suffer me not, O Lord, in Thy clemency divine, ever again to leave Thee.

Since one of the things that pleases Thee most and most deeply touches Thy heart is to have eyes that know how to gaze upon Thee, grant me, O Lord, such eyes as these, that I may contemplate Thee: eyes of the dove, simple; eyes chaste and modest; eyes humble and loving; eyes filled with devotion and with tears; eyes attentive and discerning, to know Thy Will and do it. May I, gazing upon Thee with such eyes as these, be myself regarded with those eyes of Thine with which Thou didst look upon Peter when Thou didst lead him to weep for his sin; with those eyes with which Thou didst look upon the Prodigal Son when Thou didst go forward to welcome him

and give him the kiss of peace; with those
eyes which Thou didst turn toward the Publi-
can, when he dared not raise his own toward
Heaven; with those eyes with which Thou
didst gaze upon the Magdalen when she
washed Thy feet with the tears from her own;
those eyes, finally, with which Thou didst
gaze upon the Spouse, in the *Canticles,* saying to her: "Behold, thou art fair, O my love;
behold, thou art fair; thy eyes are as those of
doves." (*Canticle of Canticles* 1:14). Thus, well
pleased with the eyes and with the beauty of
my soul, adorn me with those virtues and
graces with which I shall always appear
beautiful in Thy sight.

O Most High, Most Clement and Most
Benign Trinity, Father, Son and Holy Ghost,
one sole True God, teach me, direct me, help
me, O Lord, in all things. O Father all-powerful, with the greatness of Thine infinite
power, center and fix my memory in Thyself
and fill it with holy and devout thoughts. O
Son, most holy, with Thine eternal wisdom,
enlighten my understanding and adorn it
with the knowledge of sovereign truth and of
my own extreme baseness. O Holy Spirit,
Love of the Father and of the Son, pass on to
me, in Thine incomparable bounty, Thy whole
will, and kindle within me so great a fire of
love that no waters may be able to quench it.

O Holy Trinity, my One God and all my Good, ah, would that I could praise and love Thee as the Angels do! If all the love of all created things were mine, how willingly would I hand it over and give it all to Thee; and yet, not even so would it be a love worthy of Thee. Thou alone canst worthily love Thyself and worthily praise Thyself, for Thou alone dost understand Thine incomprehensible bounty; and thus, Thyself alone canst love It as It deserves, and in Thy most holy breast alone is the just Measure of Love maintained.

O Mary, Mary, Mary—Virgin most holy, Mother of God, Queen of Heaven, Sovereign of the World, Sanctuary of the Holy Spirit, Lily of Purity, Rose of Patience, Paradise of Delights, Mirror of Chastity, Model of Innocence—pray for this poor exile and pilgrim, and give him the crumbs of thy most abundant charity.

O all ye blessed Saints and Angels, who burn with the love of your Creator, above all, ye Seraphim who set Heaven and earth aglow with your love, do not forsake this poor and wretched heart, but purify it, like the lips of Isaias, from all its sins, and enkindle it with the flame of your most ardent love, that it may love the Lord only, seek Him alone, and in Him alone forever and ever rest and dwell. Amen.

CHAPTER 12

Certain Counsels to be Followed in This Holy Exercise

All that we have said so far is meant to provide matter for thought, which is one of the principal things in this business of prayer. Very few, in fact, pay sufficient attention to this and consequently, through lack of sufficient matter, lose much in this holy exercise.

Now we shall treat briefly of the manner and method we ought to aim at herein. Of course the Chief Master in this work is the Holy Spirit; nevertheless, experience has convinced us of the need of certain appropriate counsels, for the path that leads to God is arduous, and without the necessary guide, many go astray and lose much time.

FIRST COUNSEL

Here is the first counsel: When we set ourselves to consider any one of the subjects treated above, at the time fixed and according to the scheme determined on, we should never tie ourselves down so completely as to think it wrong to pass on to some other in which we find more devotion, more relish and more profit. Since the purpose of our efforts is to secure devotion, that which helps us the more toward this end we should look on as being, for us, the better. This, however, should not be done lightly, but only where there is a clearly recognized advantage.

Similarly, if at any given moment of our prayer or meditation we experience more relish and devotion than at another, we should pause as long as this *affection* lasts, even though it continue during the whole time of our recollection. As we have said, the purpose throughout is *devotion,* and it would be a mistake, consequently, to seek elsewhere and with doubtful hope of success for what we already hold securely in our hands.

SECOND COUNSEL

The second piece of advice is this: that one should strive to avoid in this holy exercise an excessive use of the speculative intellect, endeavoring to treat the matter in hand with the affections and sentiments of the will, rather than with speculative reasonings of the intellect. Beyond all question, they miss the way during prayer who set themselves to meditate in such fashion upon the divine mysteries as if they were studying them for preaching purposes. That tends to scatter the powers of the soul rather than to recollect them, and far from making us enter into ourselves, tends to carry us without. Thus it comes about that, when prayer is over, one is as dry and indevout and as prompt and ready for every triviality as one was before. To speak truly, such have not prayed at all, but simply composed phrases and studied, which is a very different thing from praying. They should bear in mind that in this exercise we should listen rather than speak.

In order to succeed in this work, one should set himself to it with the heart of some poor old lady, ignorant and humble, and better still, with a heart disposed and ready to feel and cling to the things of God, and not with a mind wide awake and attentive, to scrutinize them closely. This indeed is the characteristic of those who study in order to know, not of such who pray and think on God in order to weep.

THIRD COUNSEL

The following counsel teaches us how we ought to tranquilize the understanding and entrust this work to the will; the present one determines for the will itself its rule and limits, so that it may not act herein vehemently and without measure. We must bear in mind that the devotion we are aiming at is not anything which may be secured by sheer force—as some fancy. With extreme effort and with a strained and, as it were, fictitious sorrow, some, thinking of the Saviour's Passion, manage to produce tears of compassion, but as a rule, this only serves the more to shrivel up the heart and render it unfit for the Saviour's coming, as Cassian teaches. (*Collations,* ix, C. 29).

Besides, this way of acting is very often injurious to the health and sometimes leaves the soul so alarmed at the reaction that follows as to make it unwilling to face again this holy exercise, knowing by experience all the pain there is in it. Therefore, let a man content himself in quite homely fashion to do his part, standing by, as his Saviour suffers, watching Him with a quiet and simple gaze, in tenderness and compassion of heart, prepared for whatever *affections* the Master may wish to give him and ready to suffer for Him. He should rather be disposed to receive such *affections* as His mercy shall give him, than to produce them by efforts of his own; and this done, let him not be cast down when none are given.

FOURTH COUNSEL

From what has been said, we should be able to determine the kind of attention we ought to have in prayer. The principal thing is that the heart should not be cast down and listless, but vivacious, intent and raised aloft. However, though it be necessary to maintain this attention and recollection of heart, it is fitting, on the other hand, that this attention be restrained and measured, that it may not injure the health nor impede devotion, for there are indeed some, as we have said, who injure the brain by the excessive efforts they make use of to be attentive to their thoughts. Others there are who, to avoid this hindrance, remain very listless and inert and easily liable to be swept away by every wind that blows. To avoid these extremes, we must pursue a middle course, neither tiring out the mind by excessive attention, nor yet being so careless and remiss as to leave the mind free to ramble away as it chooses after every thought that comes. We are accustomed to advise the rider of a restive mount to hold his reins firmly—that is, neither too tightly nor too slack—that the animal may not rear backwards on the one hand nor dangerously career forward on the other. So [also] should we determine [during prayer] that our attention be moderate and not forced, prompt but not strained and anxious.

Very specially must we be warned against wearying the mind at the beginning of the meditation by a strained attention, for our strength is likely to give out for the remainder, just as it does for the traveller when he takes to the road too quickly at the opening of the day.

FIFTH COUNSEL

Among all these counsels, a very important one is this: that he who gives himself to prayer should not be dismayed nor abandon this exercise because he does not at once achieve that sweetness of devotion which he desires. With long-suffering and patience must he look for the coming of the Lord, since the glory of His Majesty, the lowliness of our own condition, the grandeur of the business we have in hand, all combine to bring it about that many times we may be kept waiting, pacing sentry-like at the gates of His sacred palace.

After you have waited thus some little while, if Our Lord comes, thank Him for His coming; if it seems to you that He is not coming, humble yourself before Him, knowing you do not deserve that which is not given to you, and content yourself with having made the sacrifice of yourself, having renounced your own self-will, having crucified your own natural inclination, having struggled with the demon and with yourself, and at the least, having done what you could. If you have not adored Our Lord with such fervor of devotion as you would wish, it is enough to have adored Him in spirit and in truth, and it is He who would have it thus. Believe me, it is certain this is the most perilous spot in the voyage and the place where those who are really devout are proved. If you come out of it well, all the rest will go prosperously.

Finally, if you think that really you are only wasting your time in continuing with this exercise and racking your brains to no purpose, in that case there is no harm at all, after you have done all you could, in taking up some good book and exchanging prayer for reading. The reading, however, must not be quick or hurried, but leisurely and appreciative, frequently, as you go along, mingling prayer with the reading. This method is very useful and well within the reach of all, even the simplest and most inexperienced.

SIXTH COUNSEL

This counsel is the counterpart of the preceding and must be given equal prominence. It is this: that the servant of God must not content himself with any tiny relish of devotion he may experience in prayer, as some do who, having squeezed out a little tear or felt some slight kindling of the heart, fancy that they have fully accomplished this exercise. Not thus is secured the end we are seeking. Just as a little sprinkling of water, which merely lays the dust and dampens the surface, is of no use for enriching the soil, whereas plenty of water is needed to penetrate deep down and diffuse there the fertile moisture, so [also] do we need an abundance of this dew and water from Heaven if we are to bring forth the fruit of good works. Hence are we advised, with good reason, to spend over this holy exercise as long a time as we are able, and better is one period of some length than two shorter ones; for where the time is short, it is all taken up in controlling the imagination and tranquilizing the heart, and barely have we succeeded in doing this than we finish the exercise at the very moment when we ought to be beginning it. In determining the length of time—to come down to particulars—it seems to me that anything less than an hour and a half or two hours is a short time to assign for prayer.[1] Often enough, half an hour is spent in quieting down, as we say, the imagination and bringing the strings of our instrument into

---

1. St. Teresa, Ch. 8 of her *Life,* urges two hours every day. (See also page xii of the *Publisher's Preface.*—Editor, 2008).

tune, and we want all the remainder of the time for relishing the fruit of prayer. It is of course true that the heart is better disposed for this work and, like dry wood, very much more quickly set aglow with the heavenly fire when this exercise comes after some other holy exercise, like Matins, or after one has heard or said Mass, or after some devout reading or vocal prayer. Also, in the morning, the time may be shortened, as one is then better disposed for this work.

He, however, who is pressed for time on account of his many duties should not cease to offer his mite, like the poor widow in the Temple; for where there is no negligence, He who provides for all created things, according to their needs and nature, will equally also provide for such a one as that.

SEVENTH COUNSEL

In connection with the foregoing counsel, here is another similar one—viz., that when the soul, during prayer or outside of it, is visited in any special manner by Our Lord, she let it not slip by in vain, but profit by the occasion offered; for it is certain, with such a breeze, that a man will sail further in an hour than he otherwise would in many days. It is said of St. Francis that he acted thus.

St. Bonaventure relates that his care on this point was such that, when Our Lord accorded him any special visitation, he would, if on a journey, cause his companions to go on ahead and himself would wait behind till he had relished to the full this morsel which had come to him from Heaven. (*Legend of St. Francis,* c. 10, par. 2). Those who do not act in this manner are accustomed to be punished like this: that when they seek after God, they find Him not, for when He sought after them, He could by no means find them.

EIGHTH COUNSEL

The last and most important counsel of all is this: that one should endeavor in this holy exercise to mingle meditation with contemplation, making of the one a ladder whereby to mount to the other. To this end, we should bear in mind that the work of meditation is to consider with attentive study the things of God, now busy on one, now on another, in order to move our hearts to some appropriate sentiments and *affections* of the will—striking the flint to secure a spark. In contemplation, however, the light is already lit—*i.e.,* the sentiment and desired *affection* of the will is already present, and one rests thereon and enjoys it in silence, no longer with much reasoning and speculation of the intellect, but just with undivided attention, gazing upon truth. Hence a holy doctor[1] says that meditation reasons with fruit and with toil, contemplation with fruit also, but without toil; the one seeks, the other finds; the one masticates food, the other tastes it; the one turns about from this consideration to that, the other is content with an undistracted view of those things for which it has already both love and relish; in a word, one is the means, the other the end; one the path up on which we move, the other the end of both path and journey.

There follows from this a well-known truth, taught by all masters of the spiritual life, yet little heeded by those who read—viz., that once the *end* is secured, the *means* are no longer wanted. Just as the sails are furled when the harbor is reached, so when a man after the labor of meditation attains to the repose and relish of contemplation, he should desist from his holy and laborious quest. Content with the single vision and memory of God (as though he saw Him present), he should rejoice in such *affections* as are accorded him—of love, or admiration, or delight, or such-like. The reason for this advice is that, since the whole purpose of this

---

1. The author of *Scala Claustralium,* formerly attributed to St. Bernard.

business lies in love and in the *affections* of
the will (rather than in the working of the
intellect), whenever the will is caught up and
carried forward by an *affection* of this kind,
we ought to set aside, as far as we can, all
processes of reasoning and investigation, so
that the soul may enter into it as fully as possible, without being disturbed by the action of
the other powers. Hence, a wise man's counsel, that when a man feels himself inflamed
with the love of God, he should abandon at
once all these thoughts and reflections—however sublime they may seem—not because
they are evil in themselves, but because they
hinder a greater good; and this [greater good]
is nothing else than stopping all movement
because we have reached our destination and
[are] giving up meditation for the sake of contemplation. Now this [stopping of meditation]
should take place especially at the end of the
whole exercise, after the prayer for the love of
God, of which we have spoken above: For on
the one hand, we may suppose that then the
efforts we have made will have given rise to
some *affections* and thoughts about God—as
the Wise Man says: "Better the end of prayer
than the beginning," (Cf. *Ecclesiastes* 7:9)—
and on the other hand, because after the toil
of meditation and prayer, it is right to allow
one's mind a little repose and to rest in the

arms of contemplation. This is the time for a man to let the products of the imagination slip by unheeded, to quiet down his mental faculties, to calm the working of memory and to fix it upon Our Lord. Let him consider himself as in His presence, without reasoning any further on the attributes of God. Let him be content with the knowledge he has of Him through faith and bring into play his will and his love, for with these alone can he cling to God, and in these alone is found the whole fruit of meditation. The understanding is practically powerless to secure a knowledge of God, but the will can achieve much love. Let him busy himself within himself, in the very center of his soul, where is the image of God. Let him hearken to Him, as one listening to another speaking down to him from a lofty tower, or as though he gazed upon Him present within his own heart, or as though in all the world there were no other thing but just God and his own soul. Let him be oblivious of himself and his own actions. "Perfect prayer," as one of the Fathers says, "is that wherein he who prays is not conscious that he is praying." (Cf. *Collations of Cassian,* 9:30).

Not only, however, at the end of the exercise, but also at the middle, or at any other time that this sense of spiritual repose comes over us, in which the understanding is, as it were, lulled gently to rest by the will, we ought to pause a while and enjoy this favor, nor return to our exercise till we have relished and digested this morsel. Thus does a gardener act when he is watering a flower-bed; for after covering it well with water, he turns off the hose, so as to allow the water to soak in and penetrate deeply down into the dry soil; then he turns on the hose anew, that the soil may receive more and more water and can be more richly refreshed.

No words can express what the soul experiences in these moments, the light she rejoices in, the fullness and charity and peace she receives. It is [all] there—the peace that surpasseth all understanding and every joy that this life can hold.

Some there are [who are] so gripped by the love of God that they barely begin to think of Him before at once the memory of His sweet Name stirs their innermost being. Such persons have little need of reasoning and considerations to lead them to love Him, for they are like the mother or the wife who, on the mere mention of the child or of the husband, rejoices in the thought of them.

Others there are who, not merely during prayer but even outside of it, are so absorbed and immersed in God as to be on His account forgetful of all else, and even of themselves. Often enough the wild love for some abandoned wretch can accomplish this [self-forgetfulness]; how much more may not the love for this Infinite Beauty achieve it? Grace—is it less powerful than nature and sin?

When the soul, then, experiences this sentiment at whatsoever part of the prayer it may come, let her not in any way set it aside, though the whole time of prayer is passed in that way. Let her engage in no other prayers and meditations which she may have determined on, unless they be of obligation, for as St. Augustine says, "One should abandon vocal prayer when it is in any way an obstacle to devotion; and similarly, one should abandon meditation when it hinders contemplation."[1]

A final and very important observation is this: that just as it is fitting to leave meditation for the *affections* and to mount upwards from the lower to the higher, so on the other hand, it is sometimes right to leave the *affections* and revert to meditation, when, that is, the *affection* is so vehement as to make one fear for one's health if one were to persevere in it. This often happens to those who, ignor-

---

1. The Spanish text refers this quotation to the *Enchiridion,* but I have been unable to identify the passage.

—*Translator.*

ing this advice, give themselves to this exercise and, drawn on by the strength of divine sweetness, throw themselves into it without discretion. In such cases, says a learned man, a good remedy is to incline oneself towards an *affection* of compassion, thinking a little on Passion of Christ or on the sins and miseries of the world, in order to ease and alleviate the heart.

PART II

WHICH TREATS OF DEVOTION

CHAPTER 1

The Nature of Devotion

THE greatest difficulty from which persons suffer who give themselves to prayer is a lack of all devotion; and this is something they often experience. When it [devotion] does not fail them, there is of course nothing sweeter or more easy than prayer. Consequently, having spoken of the matter for prayer and of the method to be employed, it will be a good thing now to treat of those things that foster devotion and of those that hinder it, of the temptations that most commonly beset devout persons, and finally to give certain practical instructions on this matter.

Before proceeding, however, this is certainly the moment to make clear what devotion really is, that thus at the very beginning we may have some idea of what the jewel is like for which we are struggling. Devotion, as St. Thomas says, is a virtue which makes a man prompt and ready for every good work, which urges him forward and facilitates well-doing.[1] These words show clearly the necessity and great value of this virtue. There is, indeed, far more in it than many would imagine at first sight.

We should bear in mind that the greatest obstacle there is to leading a good life comes from the corruption of our nature, due to sin. This is the cause of that ready inclination we have to what is evil, and of that heaviness and strain which we experience in pursuing what is good. These two hindrances make the path of virtue very difficult for us, though holiness in itself is the sweetest and most beautiful thing in the world and the most worthy of love and honor. To meet this difficulty and sluggish disinclination, the divine Wisdom has provided a most fitting remedy in the virtue and succor of devotion. Just as the north wind scatters the clouds and leaves a clear and open sky, so does true devotion brush away from our souls this weight of difficulty and leaves them agile and unencumbered, ready for every good work. This virtue is not, indeed, of any ordinary kind, for it is also a special gift of the Holy Spirit, a dew from Heaven, a succor and a visitation from God, won through prayer and designed to counteract this difficulty and heaviness, to

---

1. Cf. II-II, q. 82, a. 1; and Part 1, Ch. 1, of this "Treatise," where the same passage is cited. (See page 4, paragraph 1.)

banish this tepidity and provide promptitude in its place, to fill the soul with high purposes, to enlighten the intellect and fortify the will, to enkindle the fire of divine love and extinguish the flames of evil desire, to impart a distaste for the world and a horror of sin, and to establish within a man a new fervor, a new spirit and a new strength and ardor in well-doing. As long as the locks on Samson's head remained untouched, he was stronger than any other man, but once they were cut, he became as weak as the rest. So [also] is devotion for the Christian soul; deprive her of it, and she is weak at once.

So much for what St. Thomas wishes us to understand from his definition, and it is the greatest praise one can bestow on this virtue, for it stands alone as stimulus and incentive for every other virtue. Consequently, he who really wishes to advance along the path of holiness should never set out without these spurs, for otherwise he will never succeed in extricating his capricious "steed" [i.e., his own unruly nature, due to sin] from the difficulties he will encounter.

From what we have said, the true and essential characteristic of devotion may be clearly grasped. Not in any mere tenderness of heart does it lie, nor in that consolation which those who pray are accustomed at times to experience, unless these be accompanied by a readiness and zeal in well-doing. Often it happens that when Our Lord would prove His own, the one [i.e., tenderness of heart] is present without the other [consolation; or vice versa; sometimes neither one is present]. What is true is that this devotion and alacrity [willingness] frequently lead to consolation, and conversely, this same consolation and relish for spiritual things increase that real devotion which lies in a promptitude and zeal for doing good. For this cause the servants of God may, with good reason, long and pray for these consoling joys, not for any relish to be found therein, but because they serve to strengthen that devotion which facilitates good actions. Such is the sense of those words of the prophet: "I have run the way of thy commandments, when thou didst enlarge my heart" (*Psalms* 118:32)—namely, with the joy of thy consolation, which was the source of that agility.

Finally, we shall endeavor to treat of the means for acquiring devotion; and since this virtue is knit with all those which bind us in any way intimately with God, it will mean treating at the same time of the ways for acquiring perfect prayer and contemplation, as well as the consolations of the Holy Spirit, the love of God, divine wisdom and that union of our souls with God in which the whole purpose of a spiritual life consists. Last of all, we shall treat of the ways whereby we may in this life win possession of God Himself. This is the treasure of which the Gospel speaks, that "Pearl of Great Price," for the securing of which the wise merchant sells cheerfully all that he has.

Thus, clearly enough, we are embarking upon a very lofty theology, since it teaches us the way to the Sovereign Good and, step-by-step, builds up the ladder whence we may lay hold of the fruit of happiness, insofar as is possible for us in this life.

CHAPTER 2

Nine Aids for Securing Devotion

Many things contribute to devotion:

[1] Firstly, it is very important to *enter seriously and steadfastly upon these holy exercises* and with a very resolute heart, ready for whatever may be necessary, however arduous and difficult, to secure this "Pearl of Great Price." Certain it is that there is nothing great which is not at the same time difficult. So it is in this case, at least for beginners.

[2] *Keep guard also over the heart,* banish-

ing every kind of vain and idle thought, all alien emotions of love, all passionate and tempestuous movements. Clearly enough, these all impede devotion. Like the violin, if we would play on it, so also the heart, if we would pray and meditate, must be kept well tuned.

[3] *Keep watch also over the senses,* especially the eyes, the ears and the tongue, for through the lips is the heart scattered, and by eyes and ears is it filled with varied imaginings and with much that disturbs the peace and repose of the soul. Hence has it been truly said[1] that the contemplative soul should be as one deaf, blind and dumb, for the less he dissipates his energies abroad, the more will he be recollected within himself.

[4] For the same reason, *incline toward a solitary life,* for not merely does it remove from the senses occasions of distraction and from the heart occasions of sin, but it also invites a man to enter more into himself and to occupy himself alone with God, for to this one is indeed much drawn by circumstances

---

1. By St. Bonaventure in his treatise *De XXV Memorialibus,* where we read (*Number* 24): ". . . hence, it is so necessary for the servant of God to be deaf, dumb and blind, quite indifferent, in fact, to everything in which spiritual profit is not found." See *A Franciscan View of the Spiritual and Religious Life,* which contains a translation of this whole treatise of St. Bonaventure.

of place, when no alien company finds admittance there.

[5] Then, *make a practice of reading spiritual and devout books.* They serve to feed the imagination and to keep the heart recollected, and they lead men of good will to occupy their minds with what has appealed to them, for what the heart is full of is always the first to suggest itself to the mind.

[6] *Keep the thought of God continually before you,* and walk always in His presence. Make use of those short prayers which St. Augustine calls "ejaculations"; they guard the mansion of the heart and maintain, as we have said above, the warmth of devotion. Thus is a man ready at any moment to give himself to prayer. This is one of the most essential principles of a spiritual life and among the best resources for such [people] as have neither time nor opportunity for fixed prayer; and anyone who bears this counsel in mind and puts it into practice will make great progress in quite a short time.

[7] Add to this, *continuity and perseverance in these holy exercises* at the time and place fixed, especially night and morning, which, as all Holy Scripture teaches us, are the most suitable for prayer.

[8] *Practice some austerity and bodily abstinence,* a poor table, a hard bed, a hair-

shirt and a discipline, and such-like. These things result from devotion and also contribute to it, preserving and strengthening the root from which they spring. (Cf. *The Exercises of St. Ignatius: Addition,* 10).

[9] Lastly, *practice works of mercy.* In our own sufferings, they give us confidence before God; they contribute much to the value of our prayers, which can no longer be called mere arid petitions, and they secure for them a reception full of mercy, seeing that they themselves proceed from a merciful heart.

CHAPTER 3

Ten Hindrances to Devotion

Just as there are certain things which help with devotion, so there are others which impede it. Among the latter,

[1] *Sin* is the first, and not merely mortal sin, but venial sins also; for these, although they do not deprive us of charity, diminish the fervor of charity, which is practically the same thing as devotion. Consequently, we should be very much on our guard against them, not so much for the evil they work in us as for the great good of which they despoil us.

[2] A second hindrance is the *remorse of conscience*, when it is excessive, which proceeds from these sins, for it disturbs and casts down the soul, frightens it and makes it unfit for every good work.

[3] *Scruples,* for the same reason, constitute another hindrance. They are like thorns, allowing the soul no rest, so that it can neither repose in God nor enjoy true peace.

[4] Every kind of *bitterness and sourness of heart and unreasoning depression* are also hindrances, for then one can hardly relish the taste and sweetness of a good conscience and of spiritual joy.

[5] Overmuch *worry* is a further hindrance. Cares are like the flies of Egypt, (Cf. *Exodus* 8:24), which distress the soul and prevent it from enjoying that spiritual rest which is experienced in prayer. It is precisely then, more than at other times, that they disturb the soul and turn it away from this exercise.

[6] Too many *occupations* are also a hindrance, for they take up a lot of time, stifle the soul, and leave a man without leisure or heart for divine things.

[7] *Pleasure and worldly consolations,* if indulged in to excess, hinder a man from prayer. "He who devotes himself overmuch to the delights of the world," says St. Bernard,

"does not deserve those of the Holy Spirit."
(*Sermon 5, In Nat. Domini*).

[8] *Delicacy and abundance in food and drink* form another hindrance, and especially long-drawn-out meals. These are a very bad foundation for spiritual exercises and devout watching. When the body is weighed down and charged in excess with food, the soul is very unfitted to soar aloft.

[9] The vice of *curiosity* in the senses and in the intellect is a hindrance too. Seeking to hear and see all sorts of things, wishing to have about oneself things that are pretty or quaint or wonderfully worked, all this takes up time, embarrasses the senses, disturbs the soul and diverts it in every direction, and thus impedes devotion.

[10] Finally, any *interruption* of these holy exercises, unless for a good and pious reason, is a hindrance, for as a learned writer says, the spirit of devotion is something very delicate, and once it goes, it either does not return at all, or at least only after much difficulty. As a tree needs water and the human frame its regular nourishment—in default of which they wither and weaken and die—so it is with devotion when the waters of *consideration* and its nourishing force are withdrawn from it.

All this has been said very summarily, that the memory may be better able to retain it. Its truth will become apparent to anyone who is ready to give a good trial to these exercises.[1]

CHAPTER 4

The Temptations Which Usually Beset Those Who Give Themselves to Prayer—and their Remedies

It will be a good thing now to treat of the more usual temptations met with by persons who give themselves to prayer and of their remedies. They are usually as follows: the absence of spiritual consolation; the struggle with importunate thoughts; thoughts against faith and of blasphemy; excessive fear; an immoderate tendency to sleep; distrust in the matter of progress; a presumptuous estimate of one's progress; an inordinate desire of knowledge; an indiscreet zeal to attain perfection. Such are the more common temptations that beset this path. The following are the remedies:

---

1. In the Lisbon edition already referred to, there is at this point an express reference to the treatise of which St. Peter is giving a summary: "All this," it runs, "has been put very shortly, that it may be the more easily remembered. The development may be seen in the first and second part of the work on prayer and meditation, to which we refer the pious reader."

FIRST COUNSEL

Firstly, *for those who lack spiritual consolation* the remedy is as follows: Do not on this account abandon the customary exercise of prayer, though it appear insipid to you and of little fruit, but rather prostrate yourself in the presence of God as a guilty sinner. Examine your conscience and see if, perchance, it may not be through some fault of your own that you have lost this grace. Offer your supplications to Our Lord with a complete confidence of pardon, and extol the inestimable riches of His patience and of His mercy in supporting and pardoning one who knows nothing else but to offend Him. In this way will a man draw profit from his aridity, taking occasion thereby to humiliate himself the more at the sight of all his sins and to love God more at the sight of the vastness of His pardon. Though there be no relish in all this, let him not desist, for what is profitable is not necessarily always agreeable; and experience, at least, shows that every time a man perseveres in prayer, with a little attention and care in honestly doing his best, he comes forth consoled and joyful at seeing that, on his part, he has done something of what in him lay. In the eyes of God he does much who does all he can, though it be but little. Our

Lord does not consider so much a man's capabilities as his good will in doing all for Him that is possible. He gives much who longs to give much and does actually give all he has, keeping nothing for himself. It is no great thing to spend much time in prayer when consolations abound; but long prayer when devotion is slight and [there is] a growing humility and patience and perseverance in well-doing, that indeed is much.

On these occasions, it is also necessary to be more on one's guard than at other times, and more careful, keeping diligent watch over oneself and with much attention, examining one's thoughts, words and actions. Since we lack that spiritual delight which is our main oar on this voyage, we must make up for our deficiency in grace by care and diligence. "When you come to such a pass as this," says St. Bernard, "you must realize once and for all that the watchmen who guarded you are wrapt in sleep and that your sheltering walls have fallen. Your one remaining hope of safety is in your own arms. A wall is your defense no longer, but your sword and your skill in the fight. Oh, how great is the glory of a soul which combats in this manner, defending herself without shield, fighting though unarmed, strong though defenseless, struggling alone in the conflict, with nothing to bear her company but her own audacity and courage."[1]

There is no greater glory in this world than to imitate the virtues of our Saviour. Chief among these virtues is to have suffered as He did, without allowing to His soul any sort of consolation; and thus he who suffers also and struggles will be all the truer an imitator of Christ, in proportion as he too lacks all manner of consolation. This is indeed to drink the pure chalice of obedience, unsweetened by anything else. This is the touchstone showing where the refinement of friendship is to be found and marking off the true friends from those who are not.

SECOND COUNSEL

Against *the temptation consisting of importunate thoughts,* which quite commonly assail us in prayer, the remedy lies in combating them manfully and perseveringly. This effort, however, should never be carried forward to the point of excessive fatigue and distress of soul, for it is really less an affair of energy than of grace and humility. Consequently, whenever a man finds himself in this state, he ought to turn toward God without any scruple

---

1. Epistle, *Ad Fratres de Monte Dei,* attributed to St. Bernard, but rather to be ascribed to Guigo the Carthusian.

or misgiving, for in all this, there is no fault on his part, or but a very slight one. With entire devotion and humility, say: "See, O Lord, what I am: What can You expect from such refuse, except odors of this kind? What can You look for from the earth, which You have cursed, but brambles and thorns? This is the only fruit she can bear You, if You cleanse her not." When this is done, take up again the thread of your prayer as before and with patience wait for the visit of Our Lord, who never fails those who are humble. Should these same thoughts continue to assail you still, know for certain that, if you persevere in your resistance and do your best, you will gain far more ground in doing so than by dwelling in the enjoyment of God amidst every delight.

THIRD COUNSEL

The remedy for *temptations to blasphemy* is to realize that no sort of temptation is more distressing than this, and yet none is less dangerous. The cure is not to make much of these temptations. To experience them is no sin; sin lies in consenting to them and delighting in them; and there is nothing of that here, but rather the contrary. Consequently, they must be regarded as a punishment rather than a fault. The absence of any pleasure derived from them must be taken as the measure of our blamelessness. Hence, as I say, the remedy is to ignore these temptations and not to be afraid of them. When one is very much afraid of them, this dread itself awakens them and brings them on.

FOURTH COUNSEL

Against *temptations to infidelity,* the remedy for a man is to reflect on the littleness of human nature, on the one hand, and on the greatness of God on the other. Let him think of the Commandments of God without being curious to scrutinize His works, since much that we see altogether exceeds our understanding. As for one who would enter into this sanctuary of the works of God, let him approach with great humility and reverence and lift up the simple eyes of the dove, not those of a malevolent serpent, and let his heart be as that of a disciple and not as that of one ready to judge rashly. Let him become as a little child, for to such does God declare His secrets. Let him not strive to know the *why* of the works of God; let him close the eye of his understanding and open that of his Faith, for this is the instrument with which to examine the works of God. For studying the works of man, it is excellent, this eye of human reason; but for seeing those that are divine, there is nothing more completely unfit.

As this temptation is also usually most trying, like the preceding one, so is the remedy the same—viz., to make light of it. It is a trial rather than a fault. There can be no fault where the will is opposed, as we have declared already.

FIFTH COUNSEL

Some people, when they set themselves to pray alone and by night, are *harassed by terrifying imaginations*. The remedy for this temptation is to do violence to oneself and to persevere in one's exercise. Our fear increases if we fly from it, while our courage grows stronger as we resist. It is well to reflect also that neither the devil nor any power at all can devise anything to our harm without Our Lord's permission. Useful also is it to remember that we have by our side our Angel Guardian and that he is even nearer to us in prayer than at other times, for then he stands by to help us and to bear our prayers heavenwards and to shield us from the enemy, who thus is powerless to do us any harm.

SIXTH COUNSEL

Against *an excessive tendency to sleep,* the remedy is to bear in mind that this is sometimes caused by sheer necessity, in which case the thing to do is not to deny the body what is due to it, that the body itself may not hinder what is due to the soul. At other times it comes from ill-health, in which case no one should be disturbed, since there is no fault here; and yet neither should one allow himself to be wholly vanquished without just quietly doing what he can, in order not entirely to lose hold of prayer, without which there is no security nor true joy in this life. Lastly, this tendency to sleep comes sometimes from idleness or from the devil's inclining us thereto. Here the remedy lies in fasting, drinking no wine[1] and but little water,[2] keeping oneself on one's knees, or standing, or with arms extended without support, in taking the discipline or in performing other acts of austerity which prick and stir up the body. (Cf. *The Exercises of St. Ignatius: Addition,* 10.)[3]

Finally, a single and comprehensive remedy, as well for this as for all other evils, is to

---

1, 2, 3. Also, abstinence from caffeinated and alcoholic beverages may help those who have delicate systems to get their rest in less time. Plus, a good physical exercise routine can also help to sleep less, as will an overall wholesome diet and avoiding overeating. Current medical advice is for people to drink ample amounts of water each day, at least several glasses. —*Editor, 2008.*

ask relief from Him who is ever ready to give to those who know how to ask perseveringly.

SEVENTH COUNSEL

As for *temptations to distrust and to presumption,* these being contrary vices, different remedies must naturally be applied. For distrust, the remedy is to consider that in this business success is not to be achieved by personal efforts alone, but by the grace of God, which is secured all the more promptly in proportion as a man is distrustful of his own strength and confident in the sole goodness of God, to whom all is possible.

For presumption, the remedy lies in remembering that there is no surer sign of being far away [from God] than fancying one is near, for on this journey those who cover the more ground are those precisely who are the quicker to see how very much is still wanting to them. Hence they make little of what they have when they compare it to what they long for. Use the lives of the Saints and of other holy persons still living as you would a mirror; consider yourself therein, and finding that compared to them you are like a dwarf in the presence of a giant, you will no longer be filled with presumption.

EIGHTH COUNSEL

Against the *temptation which consists in an immoderate desire to study and to know,* the first remedy is to consider how far more excellent is holiness than learning and divine wisdom than that which is human, and this should lead a man to see that he ought to occupy himself far more busily in acquiring the one rather than the other. Think of the wisdom of this world, its glory and the grandeur of its aims; yet at the end, like life itself, does not this glory also vanish? What [is] more wretched than to win with so much labor what one can but so briefly enjoy? However far-reaching your knowledge, it is yet as nothing; but if you exercise yourself in the love of God, quickly will you come to see Him, and seeing Him, to see all. "At the Day of Judgment, we shall not be asked what we have read, but what we have done; not how successfully we have spoken or preached, but how well we have labored." (Cf. *The Imitation of Christ,* Bk. 1, Ch. 3.).

NINTH COUNSEL

Against *the temptation to indiscreet zeal* in working for the good of others, the remedy is to apply ourselves in such sort to the advancement of our neighbor as not to preju-dice our own welfare. Thus we should devote ourselves to the affairs of conscience of others in such a way as to have time also for our own. This time should be sufficiently long to enable us to maintain our hearts always in devout recollection. This, as the Apostle says, is to "walk in the spirit," (*Galatians* 5:16), that is, when a man lives more in God than in himself. Since herein lies the root and princi-ple of all our good, our whole endeavor should be to maintain a spirit of prayer at once so wide and deep as will serve to keep our hearts always recollected and devout. For this [profound, abiding spirit of prayer] not just any kind of prayer and recollection suf-fices, but we need that which is very pene-trating and very intense.

CHAPTER 5

Certain Counsels Necessary for Those Who Give Themselves to Prayer

One of the most arduous and difficult things in this life is to know how to turn to God and to treat familiarly with Him, and there is no advancing along this road with-out a good guide, whose warnings may prevent one's straying off it. Some of these, then, it will be necessary with our accustomed brevity to notice here.

FIRST COUNSEL

The first concerns *the end we ought to propose to ourselves in these exercises.* We should note that this intercourse with God, being as the Wise Man says, something very delightful and agreeable (Cf. *Psalms* 30:20), it comes about that many persons, gripped by this sweetness, which surpasses all power of description, attach themselves to God and devote themselves to every kind of spiritual exercise, reading, prayer, the frequentation of the Sacraments, precisely on account of the great relish they experience therein, in such a manner that the main object they have in view, and the one which leads them forward, is this wonderful sweetness for which they long. Here indeed is a great and very widespread error, into which many fall. The principal end of all our works should be to love God and to seek after God, whereas these are much rather loving themselves and seeking after themselves. One's own personal relish and contentment, that is the end philosophers propose to themselves in their speculations. "This," says a learned writer, "is a species of avarice, of luxury and spiritual greed, and it is no less perilous than that which is sensual." (Cf. Harphius, *Theologia Mystica, lib.* 3, ch. 26).

What is even worse is that, from this error, another no less evil arises, which is to judge oneself and others according to these feelings of devotional relish, fancying that each one has more or less of perfection according as he enjoys in a greater or lesser degree this relish for God. This is a complete mistake.

Against these two errors, here is a piece of advice of general application: let each one grasp once and for all that the end of all these exercises and of the whole spiritual life is simply obedience to the Commandments of God and the accomplishment of the Divine Will. To achieve this, we must die to our own will, that thus the Will of God, which is in opposition to it, may live and reign.

So great a victory is not to be won without great favors and kindness on God's part. Consequently, we must devote ourselves to the exercise of prayer in order to secure thereby these favors and to experience this kindness and thus to succeed in our enterprise. From this point of view and with this purpose before us, it is legitimate, as we have said above, to pray for and procure a delight in prayer. David did so when he said: "Restore unto me the joy of thy salvation, and strengthen me with a perfect spirit." (*Psalms* 50:14). When a man thus grasps the end he ought to propose to himself in these exercises, he will understand how to judge and measure his own progress and that of others, not by the relish he may have received from God, but by what he has endured for His sake in doing the Will of God and setting his own aside.

That this is indeed the purpose of all our spiritual reading and prayer needs no further proof than that provided by the divine prayer or *Psalm* known as the *Beati immaculati in via.* (*Psalms* 118). This *Psalm* has one hundred seventy-six verses—it is the longest in the *Psalter*—and not one verse that does not make mention of the Will of God and the keeping of His Commandments. The Holy Spirit has wished it to be so, that all might learn how every prayer and meditation, both wholly and in part, should be directed toward this end, viz., obedience and the keeping of the law of God. To stray from this is to fall into one of the most subtly veiled artifices of the enemy, whereby he would lead men to think something of themselves, whereas they are nothing.

Very wisely, then, do the Saints tell us that the true touchstone for a man is not the relish he may experience in prayer, but his patience in tribulation, self-abnegation and the doing of the Will of God, to which, of course, spiritual consolations may themselves undoubtedly contribute.

In conformity with this principle, he who would measure his advance on this path of God should ask himself how much each day he has progressed in exterior and interior humility. How does he take insults from another? How ready is he to pardon the weaknesses of others? How prompt to succor the needs of his neighbor? Is he filled with compassion or with indignation at the faults of others? Does he know how to trust God in times of adversity? How does he control his tongue? How does he guard his affections? Does he keep his body in subjection—and all its cravings and his senses? To what extent does he know how to draw profit from prosperity and from adversity? How does he control himself, and what is his manner in all the circumstances of life; is it characterized by gravity and discretion? Above all, mark how far he is dead to the love of honor, of pleasure and of the world.

It is in such ways as these, advancing or falling back, that a man should judge himself, and not by what he feels or does not feel in prayer. Consequently, he must have one eye busy always taking stock of his mortification—which is the more important side—and the other taking stock of his prayer, for without the help of prayer, mortification itself cannot be perfectly secure.

SECOND COUNSEL

If we ought not to wish for consolations and spiritual delights merely in order to bask therein, but simply on account of the profit to be drawn therefrom, *much less should anyone desire visions, revelations, ecstasies and so forth,* which may be very dangerous indeed to such as are not founded in humility. Let no one be afraid herein of going against the Will of God. When He wishes to reveal anything, He knows how to find such means of doing so, that the more a man hides himself, the more surely does God discover His word to him, so much so that even if one wanted to, one could not doubt.

THIRD COUNSEL

Similarly *we must be warned to hide the favors and gifts Our Lord bestows upon us,* except only from our spiritual father. It is this which makes St. Bernard say that a man ought to have these words written on the walls of his cell: "My secret to myself, my secret to myself." (Sermon 23, *Super Cantica: Isaias* 24:16).

FOURTH COUNSEL

A man should also be warned to treat of God with very great humility and with the deepest possible respect. However much a soul may be enriched and favored by God, she should never cease to turn her eyes inward upon herself, to consider her own unworthiness, to fold her wings and to humble herself before such great Majesty. Thus did St. Augustine act, of whom it is written that "He had learned to rejoice with fear in the presence of God."

FIFTH COUNSEL

We have said already that the servant of God ought to *set aside a fixed time in which to devote himself to prayer.* In addition to this ordinary and daily exercise, he should at times withdraw himself completely from every kind of occupation, howsoever holy it may be, in order to concentrate upon spiritual exercises and give abundant nourishment to his soul. Thus, the loss occasioned by daily faults may be repaired and new strength acquired for further progress. This may be done at any time, but especially at the times of the principal feasts of the year and in periods of trouble and distress, or after a long journey or any absorbing business which may have led to distraction and dissipation of heart, in order to re-establish it in recollection.

There are also *some persons* who, when all passes along smoothly *in their exercises of devotion toward God, show themselves lacking in due discretion.* For such as these prosperity itself becomes an occasion of danger. Grace seems to many to descend upon them in overflowing measure: so sweet do they find their intercourse with Our Lord, so completely do they throw themselves into it, increasing their times of prayer, their watchings and their physical austerities, that nature can no longer support this continuous burden, and together they fall to the ground. From this state, often a reaction sets in. They overcharge the stomach, thus debilitating the head, and make themselves unfit in consequence not merely for any bodily work, but even for these very exercises of prayer itself.

Thus, a great deal of circumspection is requisite, especially at the beginning—when fervor and consolations are great, and experience and discretion very slight—in order that we may in suchwise set out upon this journey as not to collapse half-way.

There is, however, the opposite extreme, that of the self-indulgent, who, under color of discretion, keep all physical exertion at a distance. This is dangerous for everybody, but especially for beginners. As St. Bernard says, "He cannot possibly persevere in the religious life who, as a novice, is already full of discretion," (*Epistle: Ad Fratres de Monte Dei),* who as a beginner, studies prudence and, while still fresh to the [religious] life and young, begins to look after his health carefully like an old man.

It is not easy to say which of these two extremes is the more perilous, except as Gerson wisely remarks, that indiscretion is the harder to cure. As long as the body is sound, there is indeed some chance of a remedy, but once indiscretion has ruined it, the evil is beyond repair.

SEVENTH COUNSEL

Among the perils of this road there is yet another, and one perhaps greater than any of the preceding. Many persons, having experienced from time to time the inestimable value of prayer and seen for themselves how the whole framework of a spiritual life depends upon it, come to *imagine that prayer alone is everything, that alone it is sufficient to secure their salvation,* and consequently they begin to forget about the other virtues and to grow widely indifferent. Thus it comes about that, as all the virtues contribute to prayer, once the foundation weakens, the whole edifice falls; and the more a man strives to rebuild it, the less is he able to succeed.

Thus, the servant of God ought not to fix his attention exclusively on one virtue, however great, but upon them all. Just as in a violin, one string alone cannot produce harmonious music unless the others are made to contribute, so [also] any single virtue is not sufficient to secure this spiritual harmony unless the others join in unison. A single defect destroys the whole value of a clock; so also it is with a spiritual life if but one virtue falters.

EIGHTH COUNSEL

And now we must point out that everything we have suggested so far as aiding devotion is simply of the nature of a preparation whereby a man may dispose himself for divine grace. *He must occupy himself therein with all diligence, and yet not in such means as these must he place his trust, but solely in God.* I say this because there are some people who are accustomed to make a regular system out of all these rules and counsels. They fancy that, just as in learning a trade, he who carefully follows the established rules will soon become quite proficient as a consequence; so also here, they imagine that if they duly follow out these prescribed regulations, they will quickly secure what they desire. They fail to see that this is to put grace on the same level as an art and to attribute to rules and human devices what is a pure gift coming to us from the mercy of Our Lord.

Consequently, it is not fitting to treat this matter as a work of mere human endeavor, but as a work of grace. Viewing it thus, one can see that the principal means to make use of are a deep humility, flowing from a recognition of one's own misery, and a very great confidence in the divine mercy. From this double source flow always unceasing tears and prayers. With these, entering by the gate of humility, a man obtains by humility what he is seeking, with humility he preserves it, and with humility he rejoices in it, placing not one single point of confidence either in the method of his exercises or in anything that is his own.

A Brief Instruction for
Those Who are Beginning
To Serve Our Lord[1]

AS every human art has its elementary principles, which form as it were the ABC's by which one begins, so is it also with this progress toward God, which is the art of arts and the whole purpose of life. It will be a good thing, then, to point out these principles briefly for the benefit of those who wish to enter upon it. The first steps in anything are always comparatively easy, so it will be wise to begin by indicating those spiritual exercises which present but little difficulty and are as the milk in this process of spiritual nourishment. Just as fish can only live in water, so an interior life can only be maintained by means of spiritual exercises.

To begin with, *a man must first make up his mind to serve God and to abandon a worldly life,* and for this purpose make a General Confession of all the sins of his past life.

---

1. This *Brief Instruction* and the *Three Things* are found in the Lisbon edition, c. 1558.

With this end in view, he should set aside a few days in order to go back over the various stages of his past life, recalling all the Commandments of the divine law and, with sorrow and bitterness of heart, examining into all he has said, done or thought against God, his neighbor and himself. He should then go to Confession to his own proper confessor, putting pen to paper, if need be, in order to assist the weakness of memory. And here a good spiritual director should teach his penitent how to examine his conscience and prepare himself and make his Confession, both the General Confession and the ordinary ones, which ought to be more detailed. It is not easy to get to know oneself and to make one's Confession with fruit, unless one has advice and guidance on the subject.

The second thing to do is to apply oneself to the meditations outlined above, especially to those of the first week—which are better adapted for this stage—disposing the heart by their means to sorrow and to a detestation of sin, to the fear of God and to contempt for the world. This is the most opportune moment for the director to explain the method of prayer and meditation and to develop all the suggestions indicated already. He should be very precise in providing nourishment and should know how to instruct well, that thus from the hands of a competent director, the disciple may come forth thoroughly instructed.

The third point lies in instructing the disciple as to the great respect and devotion with which he should prepare himself a day or so beforehand for Holy Communion, with what fear and trembling he ought to approach, with what devotion he should, at the last, recollect himself in order to embrace the Lord he is receiving, casting himself at His feet and thanking Him for such a visit and for so great a favor. He should understand also how recollected and calm he should be that day, and the day preceding, and in what sort of reading, meditation and prayer he should occupy himself in order the better to prepare himself for this mystery and profit thereby.

The fourth point is *to teach the manner in which a man should bear himself in all places and at all times and in all his exterior occupations;* with what sobriety and becomingness he should take his meals at table; what devotion and respect he should have when assisting at Mass and when he receives the Most Holy Sacrament; how with reverent attention he should assist at the Divine Offices, preparing himself beforehand by prayer and recollection of heart and while they are in progress, striving energetically to banish every importunate fantasy of the imagination with which the enemy then, more than at any other time, assails us.

Instruct the newcomer, also, how to be restrained in all his movements, watchful over his eyes, measured in his words, restrained in his laughter, humble before his superiors, kindly with those below him, courteous toward his equals, full of sympathy with the poor, compassionate toward the infirm, and in nothing whatsoever [to be] either hasty or inconsiderate.

Teach him, moreover, how to walk in the presence of God, having Him ever before his eyes as Judge and Witness of his life, so that he gives as much time and devout attention to every duty as he would if he saw God actually present before him.

Then *instruct him as to how to live always enclosed and hidden within his heart,* and how at all times and places and in every kind of business he should steal his mind away and lift it up to God by a little prayer, using everything he sees or hears as an occasion for so doing, like the bees who from every flower take at least something for the making of their honey. Particularly, is it a very praiseworthy custom, after the example of St. Bartholomew, to kneel down often by day and by night, or even to stand upright or in any other posture, and to pray to God, joining one's hands and *offering oneself to Our Lord with all one's desires, and begging of Him His love and His grace,* even though the whole takes no longer than one *Credo* or two. Many a time, from a devout practice like this, a more plentiful profit is derived than one can even imagine. It serves to keep alive the fire on the altar, feeding it with all these considerations and devout prayers, which are as the sustenance of devotion and of the love of God. Should the mind wander away at times, it should be gathered again and brought back to itself, but without any of that anxious effort which is so common; rather with love and devoutly, for as the Saints tell us, all these negligences fade to nothing and are consumed in the fire of divine love. Then may one, turning toward himself, gently blame himself, saying: "Where have I been, O Good Jesus; how does it come that I have drawn apart from Thee? Whither hast thou flown, my Soul?" And what hast thou won but distractions and tepidity? Knowest thou not that Our Lord is with those who live recollected and that He draws away from those who draw away from the seclusion of their own hearts?"

A man should do his best at all times to be as recollected as possible, but particularly on waking in the morning he should try to close the door to every kind of worldly thought, filling the mansion of his mind with the memory of Our Lord and straightway offering to Him the first-fruits of the day. There are three things he may then proceed to do: *Firstly,* to give thanks for the gift of a quiet night, untroubled by the phantasies and ambushes of the enemy, and then for all such other benefits, such as creation, preservation, vocation, redemption, etc. *Secondly,* to offer up all the actions, sufferings and labors of the coming day; all the various undertakings and duties in which he will be busy during it; and finally to offer up himself also, with all that he has, that all may be to the glory of God and that He may throughout dispose of all, as of what is rightly His own, according to His holy Will. *Thirdly,* to beg grace to do nothing that day that may offend His Majesty, and especially to beg this favor against those vices to which we are most tempted, arming ourselves against them by a strong determination and by watchfulness. Then recite a *Pater Noster* and an *Ave Maria* slowly and devoutly.

In the evening, before going to bed, enter into judgment with yourself and *take account of all that you have done that day, or said, or thought against the law of God,* and of the neglect and tepidity you have shown in His service, and of your forgetfulness of Him. Say the *Confiteor* with devotion, and a *Pater Noster* and an *Ave Maria.* Ask pardon for the evil you have done and for grace to amend.

In bed, settle yourself as though you were in your tomb; think for a moment what your body will look like then; say over yourself, as you would over a dead person, a *response,* or a *Pater Noster* and an *Ave Maria.* As often as you awake during the night, say a *Gloria Patri,* or a *Jesus Our Redeemer,* or any similar prayer; and each time you hear the clock strike the hour, say: "Blessed be the hour in which my Lord Jesus Christ was born and died for me. O Lord, at the hour of my death, remember me." Then think how you have an hour less of life and that, little by little, this voyage draws to a close.

When you are at table, think how it is God who gives you to eat and that He has made all things to serve Him. Thank Him for the food He provides you with, and reflect on the numbers who lack that in which you abound, and how easily there comes to you what others can only secure with so much labor and peril.

When you are tempted by the enemy, the best remedy is to hasten with all speed to the Cross, and to see Christ thereon, covered with wounds, torn, disfigured, streaming with blood. Then reflect that the chief reason why

He is there is to destroy sin; and so, with all devotion, beg Him not to allow what is so abominable and what He sought with such labor to overthrow ever to reign in our hearts. Then say to Him lovingly: "O Lord, you brought Yourself to this that I might not sin, and yet after all, it is not sufficient to keep me away from sin! By those most sacred wounds, allow it not, O Lord! O my God, do not forsake me; it is to You I come, for I see no better harbor wherein I may be healed. If You forsake me, what will become of me; whither shall I turn; who will defend me? Help me, O Lord my God, and preserve me from this dragon. Without You I can do nothing."

It is a very excellent practice often to make over the heart the Sign of the Cross, if it can be done without being noticed. Thus, temptations will be an occasion for you of often raising up your heart to God during the day and winning a more glorious crown. As for the devil who came "for the wool," as the saying goes, he goes back shorn himself.

Such, Christian Reader, is the *milk* for beginners. Now, in what follows, comes a summary of all this spiritual doctrine.

THREE THINGS

Which He Should Practice Who Wishes To Advance Much in a Short Time

He who, by the grace of Our Lord, wishes to profit much in a short time should be solicitous about three things:

The First is austerity and mortification of the flesh: roughness, asperity and temperance in eating and drinking, in one's clothing, bed and such-like; praying on one's knees or standing erect, prostrate or with arms extended; taking the discipline, wearing a hairshirt, fasting, and above all, watching devoutly in prayer; promptness to profit by occasions of afflicting the body and banishing self-love, without however injuring one's health. For this, the advice of one's director should be sought, or if one has none, then of any other person known to be very spiritual, very mortified and exemplary. Since very few understand a holy life except insofar as they practice it, should this exterior succor fail you, then help yourself with as much discretion as you can, relying upon Our Lord and not on the prudence of the flesh. One whom God favors must begin with discretion, testing here and there in turn; but experience, prayer and a pure intention end by making clear what is to be done.

The Second and more important thing is this: *to be intent upon the interior mortification of oneself,* one's desires and sensual inclinations, upon the giving up of one's own will in order to accomplish God's will and that of superiors to whom one owes obedience, and of one's director, if a person has one; to be intent upon the exercise of virtue, interior and exterior, as occasion may demand, or the obligation of charity, which we owe toward our neighbor or ourselves, or finally, as Our Lord may interiorly invite us thereto, without, however, placing us under any obligation.

The Third is to be intent unceasingly upon prayer, for it is impossible to crucify the flesh, and much more is interior mortification impossible for us and self-renunciation and the practice of virtues (which are beyond nature) without the help of Our Lord's grace. For Him, it is very easy to work within us upon our whole nature, and He will do it instantly if we ask it of Him. We are poor and have no energy for toil, but if we would be rich with the gifts of Heaven, we must, perforce, beg them from Him who will never cease bestowing them upon us, if we on our side cease not to implore them. He who would enrich himself with these gifts, and above all, who would by a special grace possess God, should have his determined times of prayer, which as has been said, he should occasionally prolong, and he should walk always in the presence of Our Lord, as we have explained.

These are the three principal things the servant of God should secure if he wishes his holocaust to be very pure and very perfect. Maintaining these three points, a man is indeed entirely reformed in all directions—viz., in soul and mind and body. By fasts and corporal austerities is the body sanctified; by the mortifications and abnegation of all its inclinations the mind is sanctified; while by prayer and contemplation the soul advances toward that perfection in which, by uniting it to God, it becomes one with Him, which is indeed its ultimate perfection.

But here we should note that, for the completion of this holocaust, two things are wanting, for the body has its senses and the mind its imagination and its thoughts. Consequently, to the three points mentioned above we must add two more: viz., *the guarding of one's senses:* the eyes, the ears and above all the tongue, which is the key of all; and secondly, *the guarding of one's heart or imagination,* that it be not free to roam at will, running hither and thither as it chooses, but may dwell always in holy considerations and thoughts. "It is not enough," says St. Bernard, "for a devout man to curb his affections, if he does not also restrain his imagination and keep it recollected." (*De Deo orando*).

To reduce all this to some order, it must be clearly understood that the heart of man, free from sin, needs help if it is to work well, as the earth does if it is to bear fruit. For the soil, we see that two things are needed: rain and dew from above, and labor and cultivation on man's part. Without these, the earth of itself can only produce briars and thorns. So also must we recognize that, as a result of sin, our heart of itself can only bring forth those thorns of which the Apostle speaks: "The works of the flesh are manifest, which are fornication, uncleanness, immodesty . . . enmities, contentions, emulations . . . quarrels, dissensions, sects." (*Galatians* 5:19-20). But if we would secure the fruit of eternal life, we must work in the sweat of our brow and with the water and dew of Heaven. For the former, mortification of the flesh, custody of the senses, control of concupiscence and watchfulness over the workings of imagination are what we must practice. It is the spiritual effort corresponding to the cultivation of the soil. For the latter we have the Sacraments and prayer. The Sacraments serve to secure for us this water from Heaven, which is grace; and the work of prayer is to beg for this, and then to obtain it as a recompense. Thus, by the intervention of the grace of God and the labor of man, this earth of malediction brings forth the fruit of benediction, provided always that our own toil is not itself devoid of grace, for from God only every good thing must come.

Thus, to sum up, *the life of every true and perfect Christian must be a mingling of unceasing prayer and work.* Two feet are essential for us on this journey: the one work, the other prayer. Let a man trust himself to God and toil with constancy for His love, but not in suchwise as, on the one hand, by a foolish confidence in God to allow himself to slumber, nor on the other, by excessive reliance on his own efforts to come to belittle the value of divine grace (as the Pelagians did); but rather, let him follow the proverb, "God helps him who helps himself."

It is easy from this to see that really the Christian life is nothing else than one long cross and one long prayer. When I say "cross," understand it of the whole of man with all his powers, for all have been crippled by sin and all need the touch of reforming steel. Thus must there be a cross for the body and another for the eyes; one for the ears and another for the tongue; one for the affections and sensual appetites, another for the imagination. All these crosses are necessary. This is that pain and death which our soul ought to choose and embrace in order that, dead to the life of the first Adam, it may live with the life of the Second. Without this cross, our prayers are of no value, except to involve us deeper in error; for toil avails us nothing without prayer, since it achieves nothing durable; and prayer without toil is profitless, since it bears no fruit.

With these two qualifications, we shall become the living temple of God, for He has two sanctuaries: the one of "sacrifice," (*2 Paralipominon* 7:12), the other of "prayer." (Cf. *Luke* 19:46). With these we shall go to "the mountain of myrrh and to the hill of frankincense," (*Canticle of Canticles* 4:6), ascending the slopes by way of the sweetness of prayer and the bitterness of mortification.

PAX ANIMAE

"Peace I leave with you, my peace I give unto you: not as the world giveth, do I give unto you. Let not your heart be troubled, nor let it be afraid."

—John 14:27

TRANSLATOR'S INTRODUCTION

Pax Animae: A Question of Authorship[1]

IN England, not a few readers are already acquainted with the exquisite little spiritual treatise entitled *Pax Animae* [*Peace of Soul*], in which is declared how necessary are peace and tranquility for the soul and how they may be obtained. In comparatively recent years, though not for the first time, the little book was brought to the notice of English readers by the Benedictine monk, Dom Jerome Vaughan. The author is given as "Saint Peter Alcantara," and the work appears "from an old English translation of 1665." There is a very beautiful dedication "To the Right Rev. and Religious Lady, Mother Bridget More, Prioress of the English Benedictine Nuns at Paris," which appears over the original translator's initials, T. W., 1665.

The work as edited by Dom Jerome Vaughan was deservedly popular and went into four editions. It is perhaps worthwhile mentioning that *A Short Treatise of the Three*

---

1. This Introduction is almost exclusively based on P. Ubald d'Alençon's *Note,* prefixed to his French translation of this work: Paris, 1912.

Principal Virtues and Vows of Religious Persons, which Dom Vaughan included in the same little volume with *Pax Animae,* and which is innocently ascribed by the original translator to the "Rev. F. Geronimo de Ferrara," is nothing else than a very beautiful letter of the redoubtable Dominican, Savonarola (Girolamo Savonarola—1452-1498), written to Magdalen Pica, Countess of Mirandola, concerning her design of entering into the Order of St. Clare. Here it would seem is an instance of a case where, consciously or unconsciously, the name of an author likely in some quarters to cause alarm is disguised, or at least not emphasized. In the case of *Pax Animae,* we have possibly, at least, an instance of the much more common practice in old days of ascribing to some well-known and universally esteemed personage the authorship of a work whose true author had somehow been lost sight of. The real author of *Pax Animae* would seem to be, not St. Peter of Alcantara, but Friar John of Bonilla.

The original work was in Spanish and was first published at Alcala under the title *Tratado de quan necessaria sea la Paz de l'Alma, y como se puede alcanza—Treatise on What is Necessary for Peace of Soul and How It Can Be Attained.* This was in 1580, eighteen years after the death of St. Peter of

Alcantara. In 1597 appeared the first translation of the *Treatise*. It was a version in Italian, *La Pace dell' Anima. . . . Opera del R. P. Fra Giovanni di Boniglia dell' Ordine Osservante di San Francesco*—*Peace of Soul . . . A Work of R. P. Friar John of Bonilla of the [stricter] Observant Order of St. Francis.* At the opening of the seventeenth century appear the first French translations—in which the author of the work is again stated to be John of Bonilla—that of 1604, and that of 1625, *Brief traiété où est déclaré combien est nécessaire la Paix de l'âme . . . par le R. P. Fr. Jean de Bonilla de l'Ordre de l'Observance de Saint François*—*A Brief Treatise Wherein Is Explained How Peace of Soul Is Necessary . . .* by The Reverend Priest Fr. John of Bonilla of the Order of [stricter] Observance of St. Francis. These were published at Rouen. In 1646 there appeared another French translation at Paris, ascribed to *Jean de Bovilla,* the *v* for the *n* being an obvious typographical error. The Latin translations begin for certain in 1662. In that year there appeared at Paris the *Tractatus de pace animae*—*Treatise on Peace of Soul*—which three years later was incorporated together with the well-known *Pugna Spiritualis,* or *Spiritual Combat,* in a collection of spiritual writings, under the general title, *Opus spirituale*—*Spiritual Work.* In this work the *Tractatus* appears without any author's name. Before the century is out, it is already appearing *"as the work of the Theatine, Scupoli,"* who wrote, so it is thought, the *Spiritual Combat.* A hardly recognizable version of *Peace of Soul* does in fact still appear in the editions of the *Spiritual Combat* published some years back in Dublin, and innumerable French editions of the last century combine the two works in one volume. No one nowadays, however, attributes *Pax Animae* to Scupoli; it would be truer to attribute the *Spiritual Combat* to the author of *Pax Animae,* for, that the latter work formed a kind of Franciscan source of the *Spiritual Combat* has been, I fancy, adequately established in the *Etudes Franciscaines,* Vol. xxvii.

From the foregoing, the claim of John de Bonilla to the authorship of *Pax Animae* would really seem to be incontestable. How then has the work ever come to be attributed to St. Peter? Frankly, I know of no grounds whatever except the title-page of Dom Jerome Vaughan's edition. This clearly is far from affirming there *are* no grounds, but so far I know of none. The as yet unidentified T. W., who is responsible for the old English version of 1665, gives no indication in his long introductory dedication that he thought of St. Peter as the author of this "devout treatise from Spain." If T. W. is unidentified, so also is his English translation, of which no manuscript or other original copy appears available. The only other English translation I know of is *The Quiet of the Soul,* edited by the Rev. Fr. Collins, which appeared in London in 1876 and of which there is a copy in the British Museum. Here John of Bovilla (*sic*) is given as the author.

As to John himself, only the slenderest information is forthcoming. He was a Spanish Franciscan of the Observance and lived in the sixteenth century, so we may group him at once with the magnificent cluster of Spanish saints and spiritual writers which that century produced. In 1581 he was superior of the Observant convent of Villasilos, a house belonging to that Province of the Conception which at a subsequent date numbered among its sons the Englishmen, Nicholas Day, Francis Bell and John Baptist Bullaker. That John of Bonilla met all these three is by no means a far-fetched supposition, for according to the *Table universelle des auteurs ecclesiastiques* ("Universal List of Church Authors") of Dupin (Paris, 1704), John was still living in 1630. By none who read his treatise—quiet, consoling, and yet so full of strength—is he ever likely to be forgotten.

The following version is, with one or two

slight alterations, identical with that published by Dom Jerome Vaughan. The original text seems to have undergone so many verbal changes as hardly to justify the abandonment of the very beautiful old English version of 1665. Two undoubtedly authentic chapters omitted from that version have however been inserted, and the translation of these is based on the French text as edited by P. Ubald d'Alençon, O.S.F.C.

St. Peter's *Treatise on Prayer and Meditation,* and the *Pax Animae* form part[1] of the Franciscan contribution to that great volume of spiritual literature for which the world is indebted to sixteenth-century Spain.

—Dominic Devas, O.F.M.

---

1. "Part," for we must not forget Diego de Estella's *Meditations on the Love of God,* so prized by the martyr, Ven. Robert Southwell, S.J., that he made an English translation of them for his own and others' use. This was edited by Fr. Morris, S.J. in 1873, and an independent translation by Pereira appeared in 1898. *Vanidad del mundo,* "at least five times printed in English between 1584 and 1622," is also from the pen of de Estella. (See *The Month,* November, 1925.)

CHAPTER 1

On the Nature of Our Heart and How it May be Governed

YOU are to understand that God hath given you a noble heart, created only to love Him, to unite [with] and, as it were, to melt and incorporate itself into Him. By love you may bring it to do whatsoever you please; and as on the one side, being enamored of virtue, the hardest things become easy and pleasant to you, so on the other, if by your own strength, without love, you attempt anything, be it ever so little, you shall find it not only difficult, but altogether impossible. First, therefore, establish firmly the bent and inclination of your heart, that whatsoever you do externally may have its root and principle in the interior; for though penance and austerities are commendable, used with discretion according to every one's necessity and condition, yet shall you never thereby arrive at true virtue if they are not founded on and regulated by the interior, but rather grasp at vanity and the empty shadow of glory. "A continual warfare is the life of man upon earth," saith holy Job, (Cf. *Job* 7:1), and in order to [achieve] the good success thereof, you must always stand upon your guard and watch, which watching consists in subduing, pacifying and quieting all the movements of the soul, so that whatsoever tempest of passion or breath of sensuality begins to arise, you immediately calm it before it hath produced any disorder there. Be sure you do this upon even the least disturbance, either in or out of prayer, and then shall you know how to pray as you ought when you have thus learned to act and discharge the duty of your station. And this must be done, not with force, but with sweetness, since nothing is more opposite to peace of spirit than violence.

CHAPTER 2

On the Care the Soul Must Take To Pacify Itself

Place then above and before all things this peaceful watch upon your senses, and without any violence; yea, on the contrary, with much serenity and security, and it will carry you on to great achievements. With this peace sent by

God you will be able to watch, pray, obey and suffer all injuries without difficulty or the least repining; and though till you arrive at this, for the lack of experience, you may encounter hardships enough, yet shall your soul find much consolation besides, and every day gain new advantages and acquire new skill to make a better defense in the future. If at any time you are in more than ordinary distress, so that this peace seems to have fled from you, have immediate recourse to prayer and persevere therein in imitation of Christ our Redeemer, who to give us an example, prayed thrice in the Garden to His Eternal Father that we might not go about seeking any other remedy or cease making use of this one till we find our wills entirely pacified and conformed to the will of God. And if the temptation or disorder found you employed in corporal exercise, be not too eager to persist or strive too much to finish the same in a set time, but proceed calmly and moderately, reflecting that it is your principal affair to have God always before your eyes with great tranquility, with little regard to give consideration to any but Him. And if any other consideration should mingle and insinuate itself, you shall soon perceive the storm and disquiet it will raise in your soul; and by thus rising and falling you will come clearly to dis-cover that all our misery is from self-love, while we wish to have all things our own way and discompose ourselves when we fail therein.

CHAPTER 3

How by Little and Little We Are to Build This Habitation of Peace

Have a care never to permit your heart to become sad, concerned or solicitous for whatsoever happens; but let your whole endeavor be to keep and preserve this peace, since Our Lord tells us, "Blessed are the peacemakers." (*Matthew* 5:9). Doing thus, He will come and build Himself a city of peace in your soul, a house of delights. He requires no more on your part but that, as often as your senses mutiny, you hasten to repress and quiet them, stilling all your powers, movements, thoughts and actions. But as a city is not built in one day, so neither in one day ought you to pretend to this internal peace, it being no less than to build a house for God and a temple for His Holy Spirit, although indeed He be the principal Architect and without Him all your labor were in vain. Now the cornerstone and chief foundation stone of this structure is humility.

CHAPTER 4

To Purchase this Peace, the Soul Must Renounce all Other Comforts

That this important foundation of humility may be solidly and durably laid, you must endeavor to embrace with open arms and sisterly affection all tribulations, desiring to be condemned and vilified by all the world and to have no comforter but only God. The judgment and maxim which must take firm root in and absolute possession of your soul is this: That God alone is all your joy and welfare; all things else to you are nothing other than thorns and briers. Accustom your soul to entertain itself with God. Think that if you were being borne along to receive some affront or confusion, with what content and alacrity you would go, suffering with joy in His presence and for His love, valuing and seeking no other honor whatsoever but to suffer for Him and His glory. When any reprehension, injury or contempt befalls you, cherish it as a hidden and an unknown treasure, as a purifying expiation for all your former transgressions. Desire not in this life the affection or esteem of any creature. Let nobody make any account of you, or so much as take notice that there is such a person in existence as yourself, but as [rendering you] the greatest of kindnesses, leave you to suffer with Christ crucified. And above all, defend yourself against yourself as against the worst of enemies; never follow your own will, judgment or inclination, unless you willfully seek your own ruin; and when your affection or inclination leads you to anything, though it be ever so holy, represent it purely, with profound humility, in the sight of God, beseeching Him to bring to pass His own holy will in it as He sees good, and this with sincerity and with fervor of heart, without any mixture of self-love, knowing that of yourself you are nothing, have nothing, nor can secure yourself against those desires and judgments which have the appearance of sanctity, peace and indiscreet zeal, of which Our Lord saith: "Beware of false prophets, who come to you in the clothing of sheep, but inwardly they are ravening wolves. By their fruits you shall know them." (*Matthew* 7:15-16). The fruit of such temptations is to leave in the soul disquiet and dissatisfaction. Whatsoever withdraws from humility, from internal peace and tranquillity, be the pretext ever so specious, is a false prophet and a ravenous wolf, which under the cover of the sheep's clothing, comes to deprive you of the virtues most essential to your advancement, and in a moment to devour what with much time and industry you have built up. By how much more appearance of sanctity the thing hath, so much the more strictly doth it require to be examined—but still, without violation of your interior peace and tranquillity, as hath been said. And if at any time you fail in these directions, trouble not, but rather, humble yourself before Our Lord, acknowledging your own weakness, and take heed for the future; perhaps it was permitted to abase and quell some secret pride which you were not aware of. And if, moreover, the sparks of extinct vices or concupiscences revive now and then and threaten your soul, be not dismayed, but redouble your watch, and gently withdraw your spirits and settle them in peace, neither afflicting yourself, nor rejoicing, nor growing angry, but preserving your soul pure and calm for the operation of God, whom you will certainly find within your own breast, and be by Him convinced that the divine aim is always at your good and profit, though you have ever so much difficulty to apprehend it in the aforesaid cases.

CHAPTER 5

How the Soul is to Keep Itself Solitary, that God May Work in It

You cannot make too much account of your soul, where God resides and delights Himself. Set so high a value upon it as to disdain and scorn to permit anything else to enter in and defile it. Let your whole expectation and longing be fixed on the coming of your Lord, who desires to find in it this free and happy disposition, without any other thought, any other wish, any other will or tendency. Out of your own head, seek not without the advice of your spiritual Father crosses which you may pretend to suffer for God; but let God dispose of you to suffer for His sake what and how *He* pleases. Do not *you* do what you have a mind to, but let God do in you what He hath a mind to. Let your will in all respects be at free liberty, your affections perfectly disengaged; wish no one thing more than another; but if you needs must, let it be in such a manner that if not it, but the contrary were to happen, you would experience no repulsion but equal satisfaction. True liberty is in this: To adhere to nothing, to have no dependence, no bias. God works not His wonders but in a soul thus solitary and disinterested. Happy solitude where the walls of Jerusalem are built up—desert of pleasure, banishment above all fruition of friends and country, where God Himself is so securely enjoyed! "Take nothing with you for this journey; put off your shoes, for it is holy ground; salute no man by the way; let the dead bury their dead." (Cf. *Matthew* 10:9-10; cf. *Exodus* 3:5; *Luke* 10:4; *Matthew* 8:22). To the land of the living you are travelling; let nothing mortal bear you company.

CHAPTER 6

On the Discretion to be Used in the Love of Our Neighbor, That it May Not Prejudice this Peace

Experience will inform you that this is the ready way to eternity, for immediately charity—and that is the love of God and of your neighbor—will pour itself into your soul. Christ assures us that He came "to cast fire on the earth," and desires nothing, "only that it be kindled." (Cf. *Luke* 12:49). But though the love of God hath no limit, yet that toward our neighbor hath a limit and must not exceed its bounds, lest to edify others, we destroy ourselves. Never do any action merely for example's sake, for instead of uncertain gain to them [others], you will bring undoubted loss upon yourself. Do all things with simplicity and purity, with no other design than to render yourself acceptable to God. Humble yourself in all your works, and you shall come to understand how little you can profit anyone by them of yourself. Consider that zeal for souls cannot justify or recompense the loss of your own peace. Have a longing desire that all may comprehend this truth which you have attained and inebriate themselves with this precious wine which God so freely promises *gratis* to all. This thirst for your neighbor's good is commendable indeed, since you have received it from the hand of Our Lord, not acquired it by your own solicitude or indiscreet zeal. God must plant it in your heart and reap it when He pleases. Do not you presume to till or sow, but keep the field of your soul free and well weeded, and let God sow it in His good season. He desires to find your soul stripped and disengaged, that He may engage, unite and firmly bind it to Himself. Let Him make choice of you for His workman; sit down, and with a holy idleness and a disengaged mind, await till He hire you. Abandon all solicitude and steer your course alone and unencumbered, that God may clothe you with Himself, who will give you what it cannot enter into your thought to desire, if forgetting yourself, your soul live only to His love. Thus it will come to pass that with all diligence, or to speak more properly, without any diligence at all on your part, which may in the least discompose your quiet, you will be able to calm and pacify all your transports and fervors with much moderation, God preserving in you all peace and tranquillity. Thus to be silent is to pierce Heaven with your cries; thus to be idle is the happiest and most gainful of businesses, uniting the soul with God and disuniting it from all other objects. And this must pass without your thinking that you on your part do anything excepting through His grace, where God must do all; who desires nothing from you in this silent pasture but that you humble yourself before Him and offer Him a heart disengaged from all terrestrial propensities, with longing desire that the divine Will may be perfectly accomplished in you.

CHAPTER 7

How the Soul Should Come Before God Stripped of Self-Will

Thus, then, should you go forward on your way and advance in all humility, step by step. Place your confidence in Our Lord, who calls you, saying, "Come to me, all you that labour and are burdened, and I will refresh you." (*Matthew* 11:28). And again, "To him that thirsteth, I will give of the fountain of the water of life freely." (*Apocalypse* 21:6).

This movement and vocation heavenwards you should follow always, waiting for the time when the Holy Spirit will fill you with His inspirations. As you follow this attraction of grace, you will find yourself caught up and plunged into the flowing stream of His mercy, which will bear you onwards toward the sea of divine goodness. Gather up now, to your best, all the inward and outward powers of your soul, and apply yourself solely to seek for all that can contribute to the praise and to the love of His Name. Still, let this be done in simple fashion and without disturbing your heart; otherwise, it would be enough to make it hard, stiff, self-opinionated; and the roughness would serve to trouble its quiet and even for a long time to banish it altogether.

Follow my advice. Accustom yourself—yet again do I repeat this to you—accustom yourself to dwell actually, or at least by affection and desire, in the contemplation of the goodness of God and the kind favors which at every hour He is, in His love, bestowing upon you. Receive with all humility the benefits He thus grants you.

This also is my counsel to you: Strain not after tears; strive not for sentiments of devotion; do not force your heart. Rest rather in interior solitude. Dwell therein quietly, waiting till God's will be accomplished in you. When it shall please Him to send you tears, oh how sweet will those tears be! For it is not your impatience that has secured them; they are the fruits of humility and of peace. On your part, then, you must receive them with deepest self-effacement, allowing God to work in you. Note well, that if ever you fancy this desire or the securing of these affections to be in any measure due to yourself, you will infallibly expose yourself to the losing of them.

See whereby I began and wherewith I would finish; see here the key and the secret of all this business. You must know how to renounce yourself, and with Mary, sit quietly near Christ, listening in peace to all Our Lord will say to you, without being worried, as

Martha was, who typifies your body. Take care lest your enemies—and the most dangerous is yourself—make you stir out from this blessed silence.

Be assured also of this, that when on the wings of thought and desire you long to mount straight upwards to God and to rest in Him, you should set no term nor limit to your vision of Him, fashioning Him to your imagination according to the semblance of earthly things; rather, as Incomparable Immensity should you represent Him to yourself, a Power without limit, an Entity without bounds, an Infinite Being, Wonder unfathomable. Such be the subject of your contemplation—or rather, of your admiration.

And yet, everywhere will you find Him in His fullness; even in your own soul, when you enter therein to seek Him, for His "delights are to be with the children of men." (Cf. *Proverbs* 8:31). Not that He has need of us, but He would make us worthy of His love.

Such are the truths your intellect should probe and in which your will, as I have said, should peacefully dwell.

Do not fix absolutely the number or the length of your prayers, nor indeed of any other of your devotions. Bind not yourself down to do, to pray or to read so much, neither more nor less. Keep your heart free.

Wherever it shall win repose, let it rest there and rejoice in the secret sweetnesses it shall please Our Lord to grant. And if by reason of some hindrance you must give up all you determined on, be not worried thereat; brook no regrets. The end of your spiritual exercises is to relish Our Lord, to clasp Him and to rejoice in His presence. This won, the means that lead thereto must be left; there is no more that they can do.

Nothing is so opposed to true repose and peace as anxiety to achieve an enterprise one is bent on bringing to a conclusion. When the intention is set on the necessary accomplishment of this or that, God can no longer dispose of us freely nor lead us along the pathway of His choice. What is this in reality but to force Him to accommodate Himself to our fantasy? It is to prefer our will to His; to wish to please Him on one side and to disobey Him on the other; in a word, to seek Him while flying from Him.

If you wish in all sincerity to advance along this way and reach the goal you have proposed to yourself, have no other intention and no other desire than that of seeking God. Wherever you meet Him and He shows Himself to you, quit there all the rest and advance no further till He allows you. (Cf. *Canticle of Canticles* 3:4).

You should have the firm conviction that nothing in all the world is a worthy object of your thought and study, except only to rest in Our Lord.

If it be the pleasure of the Supreme Majesty to withdraw Himself from you at times, then it is that you may begin again to seek Him by continuing your practices of devotion. Continue them always with the same intention and desire of finding your Beloved again; and when you have the happiness to find Him once more, leave every other occupation to enjoy God at your ease, for your desire is won.

Great attention should be given to all these counsels. Many devout persons go wholly astray and become exhausted; they often lose much profit and calm, because they have bound themselves down to leave nothing they have begun. Perfection, in their eyes, is found in *finishing* things. And what do they find at the end? Nothing, except that they are determined to be the mistresses and owners of their wills. Poor, foolish creatures who give themselves such labor to no purpose and who, like artisans and laborers, are always in a heat of perspiration without ever winning that true interior peace in which alone Our Lord is pleased effectively to dwell.

CHAPTER 8

On the Faith One Should Have in the Most Holy Sacrament and How One Should Offer Himself to Our Lord

Work day by day at building up in your soul the faith you ought to have toward the Most Holy Sacrament, and never cease to admire this Incomprehensible Mystery. Rejoice at seeing how God gives Himself to you under the appearances of bread and wine, to make you more worthy. "Blessed are they that have not seen and have believed." (*John* 20:29). Let not your curiosity lead you to desire Him to show Himself to you in any way other than that which He does through these veiling *accidents*. Draw near to Him, not that His Majesty may convert Himself into you, but that He may change you into Himself. Strive to enkindle your will toward Him that He may inflame you with His love and teach you His most holy Will.

Each time that you offer yourself as a sacrifice to God, you ought to be ready and disposed to suffer for love of Him whatever pain or insults may come to you. Offer yourself to bear every infirmity and every sickness, every desolation and every kind of spiritual dryness, whether in your prayers or at any other time, and say that you will receive them all as good things and pleasing.

See to it always, however, that you are not the cause of such, especially today. All I mean to say is that you must welcome these aridities and little inconveniences and regard them as sisters. Your whole consolation should be to suffer with the Beloved and for love of Him.

For the rest, tolerate no inconstancy. When you have once made a good beginning, persevere in your good resolutions. By their aid— I tell you confidently—the more you apply yourself to persevere in the sweetness of this peace, the more of desire and eagerness will you have of going to the very end; and persevere to the end and arrive you certainly will. Outside this quiet, you will no longer be able to live. One hour of disquiet will be for you an insupportable torment.

CHAPTER 9

That the Soul is Not to Seek After Gifts or Any Sensible Delights, But Only God

You must always incline to choose the suffering side and to rejoice to be with those who

care for you least and keep you most in subjection. Finally, everything must be a motive
to you to direct you to God without trifling
away time on the way. When all things else
grow bitter and distasteful and God alone is
your delight, then shall you possess true comfort. Address all your miseries to Our Dear
Lord, who is the Mediator between God and
man. Love Him, open to Him your heart, and
communicate to Him all its secrets without
the least fear or reserve. He will satisfy all
your doubts; His paternal and tender care
will raise you whensoever you fall; He will
absolve and communicate you spiritually,
being as He is the Eternal Priest. When your
confessor casts you off and refuses to administer to you the Sacraments as often as you
beg leave to frequent them,[1] go with a pious

---

1. In the sixteenth century, confessors and spiritual directors
typically did not allow those under their direction to frequent the Sacrament of Holy Communion. This custom
reached its greatest strictness with the Jansenist heretics
in seventeenth-century France (whose influence was felt
for another century). But this practice began to change
under the influence of St. Alphonsus Liguori, Doctor of the
Church (died 1787), and culminated with the teaching of
St. Pius X (1903-1914), who changed the age for First
Communion from twelve to fourteen down to "the Age of
Reason," approximately seven, and recommended *frequent,* even daily Communion. In the decades immediately
prior to Vatican II (1962-1965) lay Catholics were urged to
confess every week and to receive Communion frequently,
even daily. Many did. The number who confessed on Saturday in most parishes immediately prior to Vatican II

confidence and thirst to this our dear and august Lord, who though He gave the keys of His treasure to St. Peter, still did not deprive Himself of them. As often as you thus approach Him, He will give you a true jubilee or plenary indulgence; nay, loving Him, you are become already superintendent and master of all His goods. Offer yourself then a sacrifice to God in perfect repose and peace of spirit; and that you may courageously travel on this road without fainting, enlarge your heart at every step, knowing that the greater be the vessel you carry, the more you may receive; and dispose your will to acquiesce in that which you find to be God's, not barely purposing or resolving, but working and cooperating withal, lest it befall you as it did St. Peter, who resolutely protested he would die with Christ, but soon after denied Him. Why? Because he made the said determination of his own strength, finding in himself a desire and a will, which though good as in this case, yet becomes often dangerous and the cause of great ruin when one's will presumes to think or to wish anything purely of its own strength, without the divine assistance. For your part, never fail to have a good will, but at the same time, never will nor love

---

would be the approximate number who received Communion on the following Sunday.—*Editor,* 2008.

any one thing more than another; loosen on every side the strings of your heart, as I may say, having no other aim every moment but to render yourself acceptable to God, as hath been said and must be often repeated. And whatsoever you are doing, never conclude or make any determination for the next moment, but preserve your liberty entire. Yet this is not to be taken as forbidding a discreet solicitude concerning what is of necessity for each one's state or condition, for that—being according to the order of God—hindereth not the peace and true spiritual progress we are striving to advance. In every circumstance, resolve and execute immediately what you have resolved with regard to what concerns the interior; and of the exterior, be not at all solicitous. That which may be done in this instance at least is to offer your will to God; neither seek nor pretend to more; look upon yourself as a poor cripple, conscious of your own impotence, and you will find cause always to rejoice that, at least for one moment, you are in perfect liberty, ay, a liberty which you may no less obtain at all times! In this spiritual liberty consists the sum of your perfection, and as long as it continues—and no longer—shall you enjoy a divine and ravishing servitude.

CHAPTER 10

That the Soul Must Not be Dejected, Though it Experience Repugnance and Obstacles In Itself Against this Peace

But you must expect to find yourself often disturbed and deprived of this happy solitude and perfect liberty, and the little whirlwinds of your own passions will raise up the dust of distractions and disorder, against which Our Lord will provide and send down heavenly dews, not only to allay and suppress the said dust, but moreover, to cause the dry and barren earth of your heart to fructify and produce new and fragrant flowers, which may render you every day more agreeable to God than any other soul. From this intercourse and as it were continual battle, the Saints of God reaped their crowns and victories. Whatsoever difficulty assaults you, say no more than, "Lord, behold here Thy servant; be Thy Will fulfilled in me; I know, my Lord, Thy truth cannot fail forever, and in it is all my confidence; here I am, do with me what Thou wilt; I am Thine, nor hath any other any share or interest in me."

Blessed is that soul that thus shall offer itself a victim to God as often soever as it begins to be disquieted! But if you shall not be able to recollect yourself so soon in the encounter and to conform your will to Almighty God as you desire, be not disheartened; it is a cross which Christ bids you take up and follow Him, who for your example bore it first. While in the Garden, His humanity, refusing and loath to undergo the sufferings at hand, cried out, "Father, if it be possible, let this chalice pass from me." (*Matthew* 26:39). But then, immediately returning to put His soul in its accustomed solitude, as having His Will free, disinterested and wholly disengaged, He adds with profound humility, "Not my will, but thine be done." (*Luke* 22:42). Thus you must imitate our Great Pattern, Christ, who gave Himself wholly as an example for us. Lose no courage when you perceive that oft you would be glad to avoid the combat. Persevere in humility and prayer till you have lost your own will and obtained a full desire that the will of God may take place and be performed in you. Fight manfully to the end, that nothing but God alone may dwell in your soul, though for ever so short a time. Conceive not the least gall or bitterness in anything, but pass over without regard the malice and evil attempts of others, as [would] a child, in simplicity, without the least resentment or repining.

CHAPTER 11

On the Industry the Devil Uses To Hinder this Peace and the Countercare We Must have To Prevent His Ambushes

As our adversary's custom is to go about continually "seeking whom he may devour," (*1 Peter* 5:8), so there is nothing he more desires than that you abandon this humility and simplicity, and particularly that you attribute something to yourself, to your own industry or diligence, or pass at least some little censure on others, as believing that you are more sedulous and dispose yourself better for receiving the gifts of God, and consequently in your own thoughts undervaluing some others; for the least of these things would give him [Satan] a passage into your soul, there being no other door he more desires to enter by than that of self-esteem. And if you are not extremely vigilant and with all speed return to confound, destroy and annihilate yourself, as hath been said, he will cause you to fall into pride with the Pharisee in the Gospel, who gloried in his own virtues and took upon himself to pass sentence on the vices of others. If by this stratagem he get possession of your soul, he will presently master it and lodge whole proofs of wickedness therein, to your exceeding damage and the manifest danger of your total ruin. For this cause Our Great Lord and Captain commands us to watch and pray, and this you are to do with continual wariness, that the enemy get no opportunity to divest and rob you of your chiefest treasure—that is, peace of soul. There is nothing he uses more subtlety and takes pains about more than to deprive you of this peace; for if once the soul live discomposed and disquieted, he well knows that all destruction is at hand. A peaceful soul does all things with facility, exactness and perseverance and easily resists all impediments. A troubled soul does nothing as it should; the little it endeavors is with much imperfection, whereof it soon grows weary, and in the end suffers a long but fruitless martyrdom. If, therefore, you aspire to victory and to secure what you have conquered against so malign and indefatigable an enemy, be sure you admit into your soul no molestation, even for one single moment, upon what pretense or subject whatsoever. And that you may the better discover his arts in this case, take the general and constant rule: That every thought which withdraws or diminishes your love for or confidence in God is a messenger of Hell, and as

such, ought to be repulsed and cast forth.
The office of the Holy Ghost is to draw souls
every moment to God, inflaming them with
His love and begetting new confidence. The
devil's task is always the opposite, and to
this end he serves himself of all means possible, suggesting fears, aggravating above
measure our daily frailties, making us
believe our soul hath not disposed itself as it
ought, either for Confession, Communion or
prayer, and consequently he renders it distrustful, timorous and disconsolate. The
absence of just or sensible devotion in prayer
and other pious exercises he causes to be
received with impatience, giving the soul to
understand that without it, all is lost, and
that the said work had better be left alone.
At last he brings us to so high a lack of confidence and distraction that we conclude that
all we do or have done is in vain, or rather
pernicious, whence our fear and agony
increase to that degree that we almost deem
ourselves abandoned by God; whereas in
truth, it fares with us quite contrariwise; for
innumerable are the advantages which
spring from aridities and absence of devotion
if the soul be but aware of the gracious
design of God therein, keeping herself on her
part close to humility, patience and perseverance. For, as St. Gregory instructs us, prayer

made with faith and confidence is very acceptable to God, though the soul finds itself dry and without enjoyment therein. If it persevere with firm loyalty, let its distraction and bitterness be what they may, so that it even imagines it cannot think one good thought, yet that prayer is not lost or of no effect; for this very tribulation, undergone quietly and with resignation, solicits and intercedes for us in the sight of God, and this bitterness is pleasing to Him, and if we may believe St. Gregory, prevails with and, as we may say, compels Almighty God even more efficaciously than any other exercise to be propitious to us. From this we infer that aridity and disquiet of mind ought never to make us desist from any good work, for that would be both to gratify the devil in what he most covets and to deprive ourselves of a singular advantage. And that you may the better comprehend this and not receive harm from absence of advice, where you otherwise might reap much fruit, I will here briefly recite the benefits arising from a humble perseverance in these dry and bitter exercises, that the peace of your soul may not be impaired by them.

CHAPTER 12

That Inward Temptations Ought Not To Disquiet the Soul

Infinite are the advantages which these spiritual bitternesses and aridities bring to the soul, if [they are] received with humility and patience, which could it [the soul] but imagine, it would not be so concerned and troubled at them. And indeed, it were enough satisfaction for a soul, even if there were no other satisfaction, to know that God, for the most part, sends them [bitternesses and aridities], not as subjects of sadness and dejection, but most assuredly as quite the contrary, so that we are not to take them as marks of God's displeasure or hatred and aversion to us, but embrace them as most kind tokens of His favor toward us. And this we shall clearly perceive if we reflect that they happen not but to such as desire to signalize themselves in the service of God and the abandonment of all that may displease Him. When did we ever hear notorious sinners and those who fix their rest in this world complain of the like temptations? This should convince us that they are a banquet prepared by God for His best beloved ones, and though unsavory, yet more wholesome than we are aware of, let their appearance be ever so loathsome and frightful, yea, to that degree that the very imagination of them scandalizes, confounds and even overwhelms us. Nay, the more horrid and filthy the temptation is, the more it affrights, afflicts and humbles us, and consequently the more it advances the design of God, though the soul perceive it not and therefore abhors it and seeks another way to walk in, because it would always be caressed and regaled, and esteems all else lost time and pains without profit.

CHAPTER 13

How God Sends These Temptations For Our Good

We are all naturally proud, ambitious, lovers of our own ways and sentiments and ever reputing ourselves to be more than we are. This self-esteem is so prejudicial and opposite to true spiritual progress that the very savor or contagious scent thereof, at whatsoever distance, is enough to blast all hope of perfection. This is the reason why our good God is so anxious to put us in a condition wherein we may avoid the danger and, as it

were, perforce arrive at true knowledge of
ourselves. Thus He dealt with His Apostle St.
Peter, permitting that he should deny Him, to
the end that he might know himself, and by
thus knowing, confide no longer in his own
strength. Thus, He gave to the other great
Apostle, St. Paul, that vexatious temptation of
the flesh, that acknowledging his natural
infirmity, he might humble himself and, as
the said Apostle expresses it, not be puffed up
by the multitude of revelations and heavenly
favors he had received. And in like manner
the divine goodness, compassionating our
miseries and perverse inclinations, suffers
many foul and abominable temptations to
befall us, that we may become humble and
sensible of our own nothingness, though at
present we do not perceive the advantage. For
the goodness and wisdom of God never appear
more manifest than by converting to our
advantage that which seems to us most detri-
mental, by procuring us true humility, which
is that of which we have the greatest need.
And so it ordinarily eventuates that he who
finds in himself such wretched thoughts, such
indevotions, such spiritual barrenness and
drought, imputes all to the excess of his own
imperfectness and concludes that he whose
soul is encumbered and serves God with so
much distraction and lukewarmness can of

himself do nothing, it seeming to him that none but abandoned people and the scum of the world can furnish and entertain such thoughts as he experiences; for which reason, he who formerly thought himself somebody, by virtue of this medicine sent him from above, begins now to esteem himself the vilest creature in the world and altogether unworthy of the name of Christian; and this profound humility he would never have attained if those dreadful temptations and extraordinary tribulations had not, in a manner, compelled him to it. Oh, what a wonderful favor of God is this toward souls whom He knows to stand in need of such cures! But besides this, there are many other advantages which accrue to the soul from such temptations and absence of devotion; for he who labors under this affliction is, as it were, constrained to have recourse to God and pursue virtue as the only remedy for his evil and, to avoid this martyrdom, gladly quits all occasion of sin and all appearance of imperfection; so that the tribulation which at first seemed to be so pernicious to him is now become a spur to prick him forward, to run with more fervor in the ways of God and fly more swiftly from whatsoever is displeasing to Him. Finally, the pains and toils that a soul endures by these sterilities is an amorous purgatory, and if [they are] suffered with patience and humility, as hath been inculcated, they become a matter of great reward, earning a glorious crown in Heaven. All this have I deduced in general, that it may be understood how little reason we have to grieve and disturb ourselves at these indevotions and spiritual tepidities and to sacrifice to them our internal peace, as inexperienced persons are accustomed to do who attribute to the devil or to their own sins that which the hand of God hath sent, and take the marks of His love for marks of hatred and His divine favors and caresses for arguments of His forgetfulness or aversion to them; and they go on in these dispositions, thinking all is fruitless and lost which they have done and their perdition inevitable; whereas in truth, nothing at all is lost, but all proceeds from the great goodness and mindfulness of God toward us. If they could be brought thoroughly to believe this, they would not disturb themselves, nor forfeit the peace and serenity of their minds for any tribulation or imagination or absence of devotion in prayer or other holy exercises whatsoever; but on the contrary, with new courage and perseverance, they would humble their souls before God, purposing by every means and under all circumstances to fulfill the divine will, be it in what manner soever He sees good to exercise them; and preserving themselves in perfect rest and tranquillity, as they do who accept whatever happens as coming from the hand of a most indulgent Father; and instead of repining or feeling any bitterness of heart, they would render Him every moment new, fervent and most affectionate thanks; and persevere doing thus until it becomes easy for them to perform it without the least loss of time or diminution of internal peace of mind.

CHAPTER 14

What Remedy the Soul is to Use that She May Not be Disquieted by Her Failings and Imperfections

If at any time your weakness precipitates you into a neglect of what you ought to do or into lack of caution in what you say, into passion upon some accident, into detraction, or at least into consent to hear others detract, into immoderate laughter, curiosity or suspicion, or any failing whatsoever—be it once or oftener or frequently the same fault, and that after most formal and solemn purposes to be watchful and fall no more—yet let nothing of all this trouble or discomfort you, or make you reflect with anxiety upon what is past or procure new motives of grief to reproach and confound yourself with, as concluding you shall never gain ground in your endeavors to amend; that you take not the right way to it, for if you did, you would never fall so often as you do daily, and for the most part find yourself most weak and inconstant where you make strongest resolutions and the like. All this begets sadness and dejection of mind, oppressing the soul with a thousand terrors, sometimes, as it hath been said, making it despair of attaining any higher degree of perfection, and at other times, putting down its own imperfection and weak determination as the causes. Sometimes it will seem to you that you undertook to serve God only in jest, and consequently you will be ashamed to have recourse to Him any more, or to appear in His presence—as having been disloyal. And hence it comes to pass that these scrupulous persons cast away much time in thinking and speculating within themselves as to how long the distraction lasted; of what nature or how enormous the crime was; if it were a full consent, willfully procured or entertained; if they had any desire to be rid of it or no; if at last they rejected it, or would have continued longer in it; and the more they think on it, the less they comprehend and the sadder they grow. Then comes a disturbance and confusion when they set about to prepare for Confession. After much time lost in examination, they approach at last with fear and, having confessed, find themselves not one whit the more at ease, it seeming to them that they have not told all, or at least not fully explained every circumstance. Thus they drag on an unhappy, irksome and unquiet life, ceasing to advance and losing a great part of their merit, simply from lack of knowing their own natural infirmity and the way they should treat with God, with whom (in spite of having incurred all the miseries above recited and as many more as you please), one loving conversion prevails and gains more than all the sadness, reflection and examination imaginable about the fault or guilt, especially in venial and ordinary sins. And if any extraordinary disorder happens [i.e., mortal sin], it is enough to take the advice of some learned persons, or of one's spiritual father. Nay, I will be so bold to go further and to affirm that this loving conversion and confidence in God hath not only a place in venial and daily sins, but also in great ones, if God permit us at any time to fall into them; yea, though it were frequently and that not of frailty but malice, since contrition and affliction alone with a troubled and scrupulous heart can never raise a soul to perfection, if it [the soul] be not assisted with this loving confidence and confiding love in the goodness and mercy of God. And the necessity of this [confidence and confiding] is much greater in those who aim not only to escape the miserable state of sin, but to arrive at virtue and perfect union with God; and this [necessity for confidence and confiding in God] many cannot comprehend, having their spirits so dejected and comfortless as hardly to be able to think a good thought, leading a life worthy of much pity and compassion because, following their own imagination, they bid adieu to this true and wholesome doctrine.

CHAPTER 15

How the Soul Must Quiet Herself At Every Turn, Without Losing Time or Profit

Take, then, this rule and method in all the falls you shall make, be they great or little; yea, though ten thousand times in the same day you shall have incurred the same crime, and that not occasionally, but voluntarily and deliberately; observe, I say, inviolably this prescription: That as soon as ever you find yourself in fault, you trouble not nor disquiet yourself, but instantly, as soon as you are aware what you have done, with humility and confidence, beholding your own frailty, cast an amorous glance on God, and fixing there your love, say with heart and mouth, "O Lord, I have done that which is like what I am, nor can anything else be expected at my hands but these and similar transgressions; nor had I stopped here, but plunged myself further into all wickedness, if Thy goodness had permitted it and left me wholly to myself. I give Thee infinite thanks that Thou didst not thus leave me, and for what I have done I am sorry. Pardon me for Thy own sake and for what Thou art, and give me grace to offend Thee no more, but admit me again to the favor of Thy friendship." Having done this, lose neither time nor quiet of mind, imagining that perhaps God hath not pardoned you and the like, but with full repose, proceed with your exercise as though you had committed no fault; and this, as I have said, not once, but a hundred times, and if there were need, every moment, with as much confidence and tranquillity the last time as the first. For, besides the particular service of God herein, a thousand other advantages are gained by it: time is not lost in fruitless excuses, further progress is not obstructed, but on the contrary, sin is subdued and mastered with much profit and perfection. This [understanding] I would gladly inculcate upon and persuade of scrupulous and disquieted souls, and then they would soon see how different a state of tranquillity they would find themselves in and pity the blindness of those who, so much at their own expense, go on still losing so much precious time. Note this well, for it is the key to all true spiritual progress and the shortest means to attain it.

Other necessary directions for this exercise are missing here, which I have not leisure for at present; they may perhaps follow when you have made use and profit of these. Read these leisurely and with desire and hopes of fruit; God of His mercy will give more than we poor men can think of or understand.

You must conceive that this is written for such as aim at particular perfection and are not in a state of mortal sin. For this medicine will not work upon those who offend God negligently every moment and pass their lives in all wickedness; for such as these must rather use affliction and frequent bewailing and Confession of their sins, that so they may not deprive themselves of remedy by their faults and carelessness.